The Living Word II

A Treasury of Devotions

αγαπη

Yaew Dean

march, 2021

Published by Crossbridge Books
Worcester
www.crossbridgeeducational.com
© Crossbridge Books 2021

ISBN 978 1 913946 65 4

British Library Cataloguing in Publication Data
A catalogue record for this book is available from the British Library.
Scripture taken from the New King James Version®. Copyright © 1982 by Thomas
Nelson. Used by permission. All rights reserved.

Editor: Dr R M Price-Mohr
Cover design: Richard Izzard

*All proceeds from the sale of this book will be used to further the mission of
Crossbridge Books to publish Christian literature.*

Also published by Crossbridge Books:

WALKING WITH GOD by Trevor Dearing

**DIVINE HEALING, DELIVERANCE, AND THE KINGDOM OF
GOD** by Trevor Dearing

TOTAL HEALING by Trevor Dearing

GOD AND HEALING OF THE MIND
by Trevor Dearing

MEDITATE AND BE MADE WHOLE THROUGH JESUS CHRIST
by Trevor Dearing

THE LIVING WORD (daily readings from the psalms) by Trevor Dearing

THE GOD OF MIRACLES by Trevor and Anne Dearing

The Living Word II

A Treasury of Devotions

for Christians - compiled for weekly use

by

Rev Trevor Dearing MA BD

Retired Anglican Clergyman, Itinerant world-wide Minister of Divine Healing and Deliverance

All these devotions are based solidly on Biblical truth.

A companion book to:

The Living Word – The Psalms in Everyday Life

ACKNOWLEDGEMENTS

This book is dedicated to Eileen Mohr, with thanks for many years of Christian fellowship and her encouragement to me as a writer on the Christian faith, also to Ruth Price-Mohr for editing my work despite my partial sight.

I want to thank especially Mrs Heather Shead, a member of St George's Church, Stamford, for her hard work and patience with me, having to type the manuscript from my dictation over the phone and including many of my second thoughts as alterations.

I want to thank also a hundred people who pray for me every day for my personal health and for my ministry. I want to thank Mrs Elizabeth Young again for her constant encouragement for my Christian Ministry, and for singing Gospel at my meetings.

I want also to thank my son-in-law Richard Izzard, a graphic artist, for the wonderful work he has done in designing the covers for my last three books.

I want to say again, that all the proceeds of all my books are given to the ministry of Crossbridge Books, a Christian publishing company.

CONTENTS

Preface   1

Introduction   3

Part One: Devotions related to the aspects of the nature and attributes of God

Meditation 1   God the Creator   10

Meditation 2   Immortal, Invisible, God only Wise   12

Meditation 3   The Sovereignty of God   14

Meditation 4   The Holiness of God   16

Meditation 5   The Incomprehensible God   18

Meditation 6   The Faithfulness of God   20

Meditation 7   The Grace of God   22

Meditation 8   The Love of God   24

Meditation 9   The God Who Speaks   26

Meditation 10 The God our Healer   28

Meditation 11 The Self-sufficiency of God   30

Meditation 12 The Fatherhood of God   32

Meditation 13 Psalm 103   34

Part Two: Suggested devotions on the aspects of our Lord Jesus Christ, His person, life, and work

Meditation 14 The Pre-existence of the Lord Jesus Christ   38

Meditation 15 Birth of Jesus from St Luke's Gospel   40

Meditation 16 Birth of Jesus from St Matthew's Gospel   44

Meditation 17 Jesus' Incarnation   48

Meditation 18 Jesus' Baptism   50

Meditation 19 The Temptations of Jesus Christ by Satan   52

Meditation 20 The Beatitudes   54

Meditation 21 The Call of the Disciples   56

Meditation 22 The Scope of the Ministry of Jesus   58

Meditation 23 Water into Wine   60

Meditation 24 Feeding the Five Thousand   64

Meditation 25 The Houses Built on Rock and Sand   68

Meditation 26 The Storm on the Sea of Galilee   70

Meditation 27 Jesus the Healer   72

Meditation 28 Jesus the Deliverer   76

Meditation 29 The Parable of the Sower   78

Meditation 30 The Prodigal Son   82

Meditation 31 The Good Samaritan   86

Meditation 32 The Transfiguration   90

Meditation 33 Jesus the Giver of Rest   94

Meditation 34 I am the Light of the World   96

Meditation 35 I am the Way, the Truth, and the Life   98

Meditation 36 I am the Resurrection and the Life   100

Meditation 37 The Raising of Lazarus   102

Meditation 38 The Triumphal Entry   106

Meditation 39 Washing the Disciples' Feet   110

Meditation 40 The Last Supper   114

Meditation 41 The Garden of Gethsemane   116

Meditation 42 Jesus Crucified   120

Meditation 43 The Morning of the Resurrection   124

Meditation 44 The Ascension   128

Meditation 45 The Glorification of Jesus Christ   130

Part Three: Devotions related to aspects of the person and work of the Holy Spirit

Meditation 46 The Holy Spirit Active in our New Birth   134

Meditation 47 Jesus Gives the Holy Spirit to the Disciples   136

Meditation 48 The Convicting Work of the Holy Spirit   138

Meditation 49 The Promise of the Ascended Lord   140

Meditation 50 The Holy Spirit Given for us to Witness   142

Meditation 51 Jesus' Promise of the Holy Spirit   144

Meditation 52 The Fruit of the Holy Spirit   146

Meditation 53 The Holy Spirit Bringing us into All Truth   148

Part Four: Conclusion

Meditation 54 The Holy Trinity   152

Suggested Prayers   154

Suggested Closing Hymn   155

The Apostle's Creed   156

References   158

PREFACE

This is the sixteenth book of mine to have been published in my lifetime, written now at the age of eighty-seven. I would also mention that not only have I engaged in sixty years of ministry of evangelism, preaching and healing, but also as pastor of six churches, I have sought to lead my people, with myself, into an ever-deeper reality in the Christian life. I also had the experience of conducting weekend residential conferences on 'Life in the Holy Spirit' and 'The deepening of the Christian life through prayer and meditation', at Launde Abbey (in Leicestershire) and High Leigh conference centre in the Midlands, and in churches overseas that have always been very fully attended, and seemingly, deeply appreciated.

Some time ago Crossbridge Books published a book I wrote entitled 'The Living Word' These were my reflections on all the 150 Psalms. This has proved very edifying to many Christians. Now, I am writing a new book 'The Living Word II' which is a series of devotionals.

Meditation has been a very important part of my daily devotion, and I know that it has impacted on my spiritual life and on my mental and physical well-being. I hope it will do so for you. Using meditation as part of a devotional has proved very edifying in my own life. In this way, by meditating, you will not only read the word of God, memorise the Word of God, but also absorb it into the very depths of your being. It is well worth it. You will find it a very edifying means of devotion based absolutely on Biblical truth.

I have had to defend the practice of meditation, especially for Evangelical Christians, of whom I am one, who regard it primarily as a practice of Eastern religion e.g., Buddhist monks. It is to be noted however, that all other religions, which we would regard mainly as false, engage also in prayer, which Christians regard as a Biblical way of communicating with God. It is not the practice of meditation or prayer which Christians should avoid, but it is very important to emphasise that it is a matter of on what we meditate or what we pray and to whom we pray, which separates us true believers from pagan religion. You will see from these verses: Psalm 1: 'Blessed is the man who in His [God's] Law he meditates day and night', and in Genesis 24: 63 'And Isaac went out to meditate in

1

the field in the evening; and he lifted his eyes and looked, and there, the camels were coming', that the practice of meditation is truly Biblical. So, I pray that you will find from your personal devotions set out here, for either daily or weekly use, to be truly edifying.

God Bless You.

NB: Everyone, not only Evangelical Christians, should avoid 'transcendental' meditation. This practice of using a mantra to seek to empty one's mind of everything, which leaves a spiritual vacuum, could result in serious spiritual complications.

INTRODUCTION

Below is a practical example of guided meditation using Psalm 23. This is followed by a brief guide on how to prepare yourself for Christian meditation.

A MEDITATION ON PSALM 23

**The LORD is my shepherd;
I shall not want.
He makes me down to lie in green pastures;
He leads me beside the still waters.
He restores my soul;
He leads me in the paths of righteousness
For His name's sake
Yea, though I walk through the valley of the shadow of death,
I will fear no evil;
For You are with me;
Your rod and Your staff, they comfort me.
You prepare a table before me in the presence of my enemies;
You anoint my head with oil;
My cup runs over.
Surely goodness and mercy shall follow me
All the days of my life;
And I will dwell in the house of the LORD
Forever**

'The Lord is my shepherd.' Take the first line, close your eyes and see yourself a sheep. Who is your Shepherd? The Lord God Almighty, full of love and care for you, is your Shepherd.

Further thoughts:

Jesus said, 'My sheep hear My voice, and I know them, and they follow Me.'[1] 'Yet they will but no means follow a stranger, but will flee from him, for they do not know the voice of strangers.'[2] 'I am the door of the sheep.'[3] In Bible times, the shepherd would lay himself across the entrance of the sheepfold at night with the sheep safely inside, and nothing could get in or out without passing over Him.

'I shall not want.' Reflect on any needs you may have in any way, spiritual, mental or physical, especially remember that Jesus said, 'Therefore do not worry, saying, 'What shall we eat?' or 'What shall we drink' o 'What shall we wear?' For after all these things the Gentiles seek. For your heavenly Father knows that you need all these things. But seek first the kingdom of God and His righteousness, and all these things shall be added to you.'[4]

'He makes me to lie down in green pastures; He leads me beside still waters.' Picture this scene: a lovely grassy bank, a stream of water bubbling over stones beneath it. This speaks of peace. Feel the peace.

'He restores my soul.' Have you been battered by the enemy, or in any way discouraged, or feel even God has failed you? Remember His promise is, 'So I will restore to you the years that the swarming locust has eaten.'[5] Feel the Holy Spirit restoring your soul.

'He leads me in the paths of righteousness for His name's sake.' Picture yourself on a narrow path slowly walking to your destination. Remember Jesus' words 'Blessed are those who hunger and thirst for righteousness, for they shall be filled.'[6] Have you ever strayed from this path through disobedience or sin? See yourself getting back on it.

'Yea, though I walk through the valley of the shadow of death, I will fear no evil; for You are with me; Your rod and Your staff, they comfort me.' Picture yourself now walking with the Lord in whatever illness or fear you may have for the future. The Lord Jesus Christ Himself will never leave your side. He is with you.

'You prepare a table before me in the presence of my enemies.' This gives you the assurance of victory through your faith in the Lord Jesus Christ. Remember what the Bible says and believe it. 'Yet in all these things we are more than conquerors through Him who loved us.'⁷ So do not let any fear whatever, of the evil one, daunt you in any way.

'You anoint my head with oil; my cup runs over.' This is a picture of you being anointed from the head down with oil, which is a Biblical symbol of the presence of the Holy Spirit Himself. See yourself sitting on a throne and angels pouring oil upon your head. Feel it running down you. You are anointed, at all times, with the presence of God's Holy Spirit, the Comforter that is the Divine Helper.

'Surely goodness and mercy shall follow me all the days of my life.' What a wonderful promise for all the rest of your life. A promise made by God Himself. Just wallow in it and relish it.

'And I will dwell in the house of the Lord forever.' What a wonderful, absolutely certain future you have forever, even through death itself, which is the doorway to God's House for you and any of your loved ones. Remember Jesus' words "In My Father's house are many mansions; if it were not so, I would have told you. I go to prepare a place for you. And if I go and prepare a place for you, I will come again and receive you to Myself; that where I am, there you may be also.'[8] As the hymn says, 'Forever with the Lord. Amen, so let it be. Life from the dead is in that word, 'tis immortality.'[9]

You need not take the whole Psalm at once, just bits of it as you feel led. It may take you several days, or a long time, to really feel you have obtained all these promises made by God in this Psalm. End your meditation each time with the Lord's Prayer.

A GUIDE TO A BRIEF MEDITATION

This brief meditation may suffice for when you are in a hurry, but I do hope you manage to do the longer one at least once a week for your spiritual, emotional, and physical well-being.

1. Get seated comfortably in a comfortable chair, close your eyes and be quiet for a few moments. Claim the promise in James' Epistle,

   'Draw near to God and He will draw near to you.'[10]

2. Utter a brief prayer:

   "O Holy Spirit who inspired these words, please give me understanding of them and imprint them in my heart."

3. Read the suggested passage for meditation.

4. Read my further notes on the passage.

5. Think about any sentence in it that speaks to you and thank The Lord for speaking to you through His Word.

PART ONE

Devotions related to the aspects of the nature and attributes of God

Meditation 1: God the Creator

Genesis Chapter 1: 1-7

> 'In the beginning God created the heavens and the earth. The earth was without form, and void; and darkness was on the face of the deep. And the Spirit of God was hovering over the face of the waters.
>
> Then God said, "Let there be light"; and there was light. And God saw the light that it was good; and God divided the light from the darkness. God called the light Day, and the darkness He called Night. So the evening and the morning were the first day.
>
> Then God said, "Let there be a firmament in the midst of the waters, and let it divide the waters from the waters." Thus God made the firmament, and divided the waters which were under the firmament from the waters that were above the firmament, and it was so.'

Picture primeval darkness. See the darkness. See planet earth (without form and void).

See the Spirit of God as a dove hovering over the face of the waters.

See the light being created in the sun, moon and the stars. See the light in place of the darkness.

See God creating the sun and the moon and flinging the stars into space, simply by the power of His spoken Word.

10

Think of the words where He said it was "good" - perfection.

Hymn:

> **Praise to the Lord the Almighty, the King of creation! O my soul, praise Him, for He is our health and salvation!**
> **Come, all who hear; now to His temple draw near, join me in glad adoration.**[11]

Reflect on all the words of this hymn and on the greatness and the power of God and on the most important words of the Bible:

> **'In the beginning God created the heavens and earth.'**

Close with the prayer:

"God created me as a special creation. Only God could create something out of nothing."

Meditation 2: Immortal, Invisible, God only Wise

> **Immortal, invisible, God only wise,**
> **in light inaccessible, hid from our eyes,**
> **most blessed, most glorious,**
> **the Ancient of Days,**
> **almighty, victorious,**
> **thy great name we praise.**[12]

This hymn portrays much of the being and nature of God. Take it one word or line at a time.

Meditate on the word **'Immortal'** - without beginning or end.

Meditate on the word **'Invisible'** - can't be seen by human sight.

'God only wise' - meditate on the wonderful wisdom of God in all He says and does.

'Inaccessible hid from our eyes' - because of His blinding Glory we cannot see Him.

'Most blessed, most glorious' - God is blessed above anything or anyone else in creation.

'Glorious' - God is more glorious than anyone else in all creation.

'The Ancient of Days' - existing before the beginning of human history.

'Almighty' - He can achieve and do anything He wants to do, and nothing can stop Him, so we believe in miracles.

'Victorious' - He can defeat and overcome any and every kind of evil.

'Thy Great Name we praise' - end your meditation by praising the Lord with any song you know, sing it aloud.

Meditation 3: The Sovereignty of God

Psalm 2: 1-6

> '**Why do the nations rage,**
> **And the people plot a vain thing?**
> **The kings of the earth set themselves,**
> **And the rulers take counsel together,**
> **Against the LORD and against His Anointed,**
> **saying**
> **"Let us break their bonds in pieces**
> **And cast away their cords from us."**
>
> **He who sits in the heavens shall laugh,**
> **The Lord shall hold them in derision,**
> **Then He shall speak to them in His wrath,**
> **And distress them in His displeasure:**
> **"Yet I have set My King**
> **On My holy hill of Zion".'**

This means the absolute rule of God over all creation from time immemorial and forever.

He has never abdicated and must be in all things obeyed.

Meditate on the Sovereignty of God and His Kingly rule, especially in your own life and circumstances.

Hymn:

O worship the king all-glorious above,
O gratefully sing His power and His love:
our shield and defender, the Ancient of Days,
pavilioned in splendour and girded with praise.

Your bountiful care, what tongue can recite?
It breathes in the air; it shines in the light.
It streams from the hills, it descends to the
plain,
And sweetly distils in the dew and the rain.

O measureless Might, unchangeable Love,
Whom angels delight to worship above!
Your ransomed creation, with glory ablaze,
In true adoration shall sing to your praise.[13]

Prayer:

Confess where and in whatever you have disobeyed Him and bring your whole life in obedience to Him.

Meditation 4: The Holiness of God

Isaiah Chapter 6: 1-8

'In the year that King Uzziah died, I saw the Lord sitting on a throne, high and lifted up, and the train of His robe filled the temple. Above it stood seraphim; each one had six wings: with two he covered his face, with two he covered his feet, and with two he flew. And one cried to another and said:

"Holy, holy, holy is the Lord of hosts;
The whole earth is full of His glory."

And the posts of the door were shaken by the voice of him who cried out, and the house was filled with smoke. So I said:

"Woe is me, for I am undone!
Because I am a man of unclean lips,
And I dwell in the midst of a people of unclean lips;
For my eyes have seen the King,
The Lord of hosts."

Then one of the seraphim flew to me, having in his hand a live coal which he had taken with the tongs from the altar. And he touched my mouth with it, and said:

"Behold, this has touched your lips;
Your iniquity is taken away,

And your sin purged."

Also I heard the voice of the Lord saying:

**"Whom shall I send,
And who will go for Us?"**

Then I said, "Here am I! Send me".'

Try to imagine yourself as Isaiah or in the Temple with him, and experience what he experienced.

Use your imagination to the utmost and feel with him the sense of sin, which catching a glimpse of the Holiness of God, always engenders.

Meditate on the forgiveness and commission that Isaiah received.

Suggested Prayer:

"Lord I have heard Your voice calling me to serve you. I say with Isaiah, "Here am I! send me."

Meditation 5: The Incomprehensible God

Isaiah Chapter 55: 8-9

> **"For My thoughts are not your thoughts,**
> **Nor are your ways May ways," says the LORD,**
> **"For as the heavens are higher than the earth,**
> **So are My ways higher than your ways,**
> **And My thoughts than your thoughts."**

This means that God cannot be fully known, in Himself and in His ways, by anyone outside of Himself.

Dwell on this for as long as you can.

Meditate on the vastness of the depths and the heights of the mind, plans, and thoughts of God. Realise your inadequacy in understanding the mind of God.

Renew your trust in Him in His purpose for your life and what He has or has not done for you.

Hymn:

Give me the faith which can remove
and sink the mountain to a plain;
give me the childlike praying love,
which longs to build Thy house again;
thy love, let it my heart o'er-power
and all my simple soul devour.

I would the precious time redeem,
And longer live for this alone,
To spend and to be spent for them
Who have not yet my Saviour known;
Fully on these my mission prove,
And only breathe, to breathe Thy love.

Enlarge, inflame, and fill my heart
With boundless charity divine,
So shall I all my strength exert,
And love them with a zeal like Thine,
And lead the to Thy open side,
The sheep for whom the Shepherd died.[14]

Prayer:

Confess your faults, for example maybe complaining about what God has done or has not done in the world.

Meditation 6: The Faithfulness of God

2 Timothy Chapter 2:13

> **'If we are faithless,**
> **He remains faithful;**
> **He cannot deny Himself.'**

God remains faithful and true to us regardless of what we do. Our unbelief cannot affect God's faithfulness to us.

Trace the faithfulness of God in your life and the life of your family. Meditate on the unchanging nature of God the Father.

Entrust yourself and all you know to His faithfulness for this day and tomorrow and to the end of your life.

Reflect on the words of the Psalmist.

> **'The Lord is faithful in all His words, and holy in**
> **all His works.'**[15]

Hymn:

Love divine, all loves excelling,
Joy of heav'n to earth come down.
Fix in us Thy humble dwelling,
All Thy faithful mercies crown.
Jesus Thou art all compassion,
Pure, unbounded love Thou art.
Visit us with Thy salvation,
Enter every trembling heart.

Finish then Thy new creation
Pure and spotless let us be.
Let us see Thy great salvation
Perfectly restored in Thee.
Changed from glory into glory
Till in heaven we take our place.
Till we cast our crowns before Thee
Lost in wonder, love, and praise.[16]

Prayer:

Confess any faults or ways you have doubted God's faithfulness. Reflect on your every-day anxieties that you have kept to yourself instead of trusting to His care.

Meditation 7: The Grace of God

Ephesians Chapter 2:8-9

> 'For by grace you have been saved through faith, and that not of yourselves; it is the gift of God, not of works, lest anyone should boast.'

Grace means the completely undeserved and unending love of God in action.

We can never deserve God's Grace however hard we try. It is an attribute of God demonstrated in our salvation.

Grace is the love and mercy that God gives to us because He desires us to have it, not because of anything we have done to earn it.

We must surely trust in His grace and completely rest in how unfathomable it is and how secure we can be in our lives and in Him because of His unending Grace.

Reflect on the words of Paul in his letter to Titus.

> 'For the grace of God that brings salvation has appeared to all men.'[17]

Hymn:

Great God of wonders,
all Thy ways are matchless, godlike and divine;
but the fair glories of Thy Grace,
more godlike and unrivalled shine,
More godlike and unrivalled shine."

Who is a pard'ning God like Thee?
Or who has grace so rich and free?
Or who has grace so rich and free?

O may this strange, this matchless grace,
The God-like miracle of love,
Fill the whole earth with grateful praise,
And all th'angelic choirs above,
And all th'angelic choirs above.

Who is a pard'ning God like Thee?
Or who has grace so rich and free?
Or who has grace so rich and free?[18]

Prayer:

Thank God for His wonderful Grace in choosing and saving you without any merit of your own to offer Him.

Meditation 8: The Love of God

John Chapter 3:16

'For God so loved the world that He gave His only begotten Son, that whoever believes in Him should not perish but have everlasting life.'

Note that the word for love here is the special one, namely Agape, which means, in the New Testament, a love that has no selfish interest in mind; it is entirely poured out to the beloved to the extent of self-sacrifice. All this is portrayed here in this most important verse in the New Testament.

Agape love does not come from emotions or human feelings, but from the will; it is a choice that requires faithfulness, commitment, and sacrifice without expecting anything in return. God's love is not sentimental; it is part of His character and He is its source.

The Greek word used for 'world' – 'kosmos' - in this context, means humanity entirely lost and in rebellion against God.

God so loved His world that He gave His son on the cross. Wallow and swim and, as it were, take a sauna bath, in God's love and thank Him as best you can for it.

Hymn:

There's a wideness in God's mercy,
Like the wideness of the sea.
There's a kindness in God's justice,
Which is more than liberty.

There is welcome for the sinner,
And more graces for the good.
There is mercy with the Saviour,
There is healing in His blood.

But we make God's love too narrow
By false limits of our own,
And we magnify its strictness
With a zeal God will not own.

For the love of God is broader
than the measure of the mind.
And the heart of the Eternal
is most wonderfully kind.

If our love were but more simple,
we should rest upon God's word,
and our lives would be illumined
by the presence of our Lord.[19]

Prayer:
Thank God for His sacrificial love that is beyond our understanding.

Meditation 9: The God who Speaks

Exodus Chapter 3:4-5

> **'So when the LORD saw that he turned aside to look, God called to him from the midst of the bush and said, 'Moses, Moses'. And he said 'Here I am.' Then He said, 'Do not draw near this place. Take your sandals off your feet, for the place where you stand is holy ground.'**

We read in the Bible that God spoke frequently to His people, usually with the phrase 'The Word of the Lord came to me saying', for example through the prophets, through whom He also often spoke to His people.

Sometimes, however, He spoke directly to a person, for example to Moses from the burning bush.

Be very silent and ask God to speak to you in your quietness and meditation.

Hymn:

> **I heard the voice of Jesus say,**
> **"Come unto me and rest.**
> **Lay down, O weary one,**

Lay down your head upon my breast."
I came to Jesus as I was,
So weary, worn, and sad.
I found in him a resting place,
And he has made me glad.

I heard the voice of Jesus say,
"Behold, I freely give
The living water, thirsty one;
Stoop down and drink and live."
I came to Jesus, and I drank
Of that life-giving stream.
My thirst was quenched, my soul revived,
And now I live in him.' [20]

Prayer:

Pray the prayer Samuel uttered when He was very young while he was lying in bed,

'Lord speak for Thy servant heareth.'[21]

Ask Him also to speak to you even when you are not expecting Him to do so, by giving you a scriptural text, or a thought suddenly coming to you which is imprinted on your mind.

Meditation 10: The God our Healer

Exodus Chapter15: 26-28

> **"If you diligently heed the voice of the LORD your God and do what is right in His sight, give ear to His commandments and keep all His statutes, I will put none of the diseases on you which I have brought on the Egyptians. For I am the LORD who heals you."**

God reveals Himself to Moses saying His name is **'Yahweh Rapha'** - this is Hebrew and should be translated as Yahweh which means 'I Am', that is in the name and nature of God Himself, and the word 'Rapha' means Healer.

We can ultimately see then that all sickness is caused by the Fall of Man; sin, not only in this human life but also affecting the very fabric of the world of nature.

We see in the New Testament that Jesus, who was always doing the Will of God, spent enormous amounts of time and energy on healing people of sickness and infirmities.

All the work of God, including Salvation, is really a healing work and we read in Revelation that His work is also to heal the nations of discord and war.[22]

Hymn:

'**How sweet the name of Jesus sounds**
In a believer's ear.
It soothes his sorrows, heals his wounds,
And drives away his fear.

It makes the wounded spirit whole
And calms the troubled breast.
'**Tis manna to the hungry soul**
And to the weary rest

Dear name, the rock on which I build
My shield and hiding place,
My never-failing treasury filled
With boundless stores of grace.'[23]

Prayer:

Pray for the healing of any you know that God has laid on your heart who are sick.

Pray that God will heal any sickness and infirmity that you may have. Expect it to happen.

It is God's perfect Will for you in body, mind, and spirit.

Pray also for the NHS, doctors, nurses etc., who even though they may not know it, are involved in God's healing work.

Meditation 11: The Self-Sufficiency of God

Romans Chapter 8:28

> **'And we know that all things work together for good to those who love God, to those who are the called according to His purpose.'**

This means that ultimately God does not need any help at all to fulfil His purposes.

Ephesians 3:20

> **'Now to Him who is able to do exceedingly abundantly above all that we ask or think, according to the power that works in us.'**

Meditate on the all-sufficiency of God in Himself. Trust Him that He is really working His purposes out despite everything that is happening in the world that would deny this.

Renew your trust in Him, remembering that the love of Christ passes our human knowledge; that we cannot comprehend the width and length and depth of His love, but we can be filled with all His fulness.

Hymn:

'God is working His purpose out,
as year succeeds to year.
God is working His purpose out,
And the time is drawing near.
Nearer and nearer draws the time,
The time that shall surely be,
when the earth shall be filled
with the glory of God,
as the waters cover the sea.

All we can do is nothing worth,
Unless God blesses the deed.
Vainly we hope for the harvest-tide
Till God gives life to the seed.
Yet nearer and nearer draws the time,
The time that shall surely be,
When the earth shall be filled
with the glory of God,
As the waters cover the sea.'[24]

Prayer:

'Oh, use me, Lord, use ever me,
just as Thou wilt, and when and where,
Until Thy blessed face I see,
Your rest, your joy, Thy glory share.'[25]

Meditation 12: The Fatherhood of God

Matthew Chapter 6: 9 - 15

> **'In this manner, therefore, pray:**
> **Our Father in heaven,**
> **Hallowed be Your name.**
> **Your kingdom come,**
> **Your will be done**
> **On earth as it is in heaven.**
> **Give us this day our daily bread.**
> **And forgive us our debts,**
> **As we forgive our debtors.**
> **And do not lead us into temptation,**
> **But deliver us from the evil one.**
> **For Yours is the kingdom and the power**
> **And the glory forever.**
> **Amen'**

The word 'Father', in the Greek 'Abba', is a very familiar form of address, best translated as Daddy' or even 'Poppa'.

Reflect on this amazing truth about our great and wondrous God, who can be called 'Daddy' by you.

Imagine yourself as a child sitting on your father's knee and asking your father to help you with your greatest need. Transform this into imagining the same thing about you and God, your 'Daddy'.

Hymn:

> **'Lead us Heavenly Father lead us**
> **O'er the worlds tempestuous sea;**
> **Guard us, guide us, keep us, feed us,**
> **for we have no help but Thee;**
> **yet possessing every blessing,**
> **if our God our Father be.**
>
> **Saviour, breath forgiveness o'er us:**
> **all our weakness Thou dost know;**
> **Thou didst tread this earth before us,**
> **Thou didst feel its keenest woe;**
> **lone and dreary, faint and weary,**
> **through the desert Thou didst go.**
>
> **Spirit of our God, descending,**
> **fill our hearts with heavenly joy,**
> **love with every passion blending,**
> **pleasure that can never cloy:**
> **thus provided, pardoned, guided,**
> **nothing can our peace destroy.'**[26]

Prayer:

Bring to God your greatest needs, the needs of society, the needs of the world, and pray that 'Thy Will be done on earth as it is in heaven.'

Meditation 13: Psalm 103

'Bless the LORD, O my soul;
And all that is within me, bless His holy name!
Bless the LORD, O my soul
And forget not all His benefits;
Who forgives all your iniquities,
Who heals all your diseases,
Who redeems your life from destruction,
Who crowns you with loving kindness and
tender mercies,
Who satisfies your mouth with good things,
So that your youth is renewed like the eagle's.

The LORD executes righteousness
and justice for all who are oppressed.
He made known His ways to Moses,
His acts to the children of Israel.
The LORD is merciful and gracious,
slow to anger and abounding in mercy.
He will not always strive with us,
Nor will He keep His anger forever.
He has not dealt with us according to our sins,
Nor punished us according to our iniquities.

For as the heavens are high above the earth,
So great is His mercy toward those who fear
Him;
As far as the east is from the west,
So far has He removed our transgressions from
us.
As a father pities his children,
So the LORD pities those who fear Him.
For He knows our frame,
He remembers that we are dust.

As for man, his days are like grass;
As a flower of the field, so he flourishes.
For the wind passes over it, and it is gone,
And its place remembers it no more.
But the mercy of the LORD is from everlasting to everlasting,
On those who fear Him,
And His righteousness to children's children,
To such as keep His covenant,
And to those who remember His commandments to do them.

The LORD has established His throne in heaven,
And His kingdom rules over all.

Bless the LORD, you His angels,
Who excel in strength, who do His word,
Heeding the voice of His word.
Bless the LORD, all you His hosts,
you ministers of His who do His pleasure.
Bless the LORD, all His works,
In all places of His dominion.

Bless the LORD, O my soul!'

Enter with the Psalmist into all the blessings one by one, that he, and now you, have received.

Praise God for each one, for example 'forgives all our sins', 'heals all our diseases', and 'renews our strength'.

Hymn:

'Now thank we all our God,
with hearts and hands and voices;
who wondrous things has done,
in whom His world rejoices;
who from our mothers' arms
has blessed us on our way
with countless gifts of love,
and still is ours today.

O may this bounteous God
through all our life be near us,
with ever joyful hearts
and blessed peace to cheer us;
and keep us in His grace,
and guide us when perplexed;
and free us from all ills
in this world, till the next!

All praise and thanks to God
the Father now be given,
The Son, and Him Who reigns
with them in highest Heaven,
The one eternal God,
whom earth and Heaven adore;
For thus it was, is now,
and shall be evermore.'[27]

prayer:

Bless God for all His blessings to you and to those whom
you love.

PART TWO

Suggested devotions on the aspects of our Lord Jesus Christ

His person, life, and work.

Meditation 14: The Pre-existence of the Lord Jesus Christ

John Chapter 17: 4-5

> **'I have glorified You on the earth. I have finished the work which You have given Me to do. And now, O Father, glorify Me together with Yourself, with the glory which I had with You before the world was.'**

Try to imagine and contemplate Jesus' Heavenly Glory. How big is your Jesus? How glorious and important is He in your daily life?

Speak in your mind or with your lips any words that come to you to adore or glorify our pre-existent Lord. Always keep in mind His pre-existent glory when meditating on the life of Jesus, remembering the words of the Apostle Paul in his letter to the Colossians 1:15-17:

> **'He is the image of the invisible God, the first-born over all creation. For by Him all things were created that are in heaven and that are on earth, visible and invisible, whether thrones or dominions or principalities or power. All things were created through Him and for Him, and He is before all things, and in Him all things consist.'**

Hymn:

'Crown Him with many crowns,
The Lamb upon His throne,
Hark, how the heavenly anthem drowns
All music but its own.
Awake my soul and sing
Of Him who died for thee
And hail Him as they matchless King
Through all eternity.

Crown Him the Lord of years,
The Potentate of time,
Creator of the rolling spheres
Ineffably sublime.
All hail, Redeemer, hail.
For Though hast died for me.
Thy praise shall never, never fail
Throughout eternity.' [28]

Prayer:

Praise God for revealing His glory through His Son. Thank Him for specific things in His creation that move you to glorify His works.

Meditation 15: Birth of Jesus from St Luke's Gospel

Luke Chapter 2: 8 -20

'Now there were in the same country shepherds living out in the fields, keeping watch over their flock by night. And behold, an angel of the Lord stood before them, and the glory of the Lord shone around them, and they were greatly afraid. Then the angel said to them,
"Do not be afraid, for behold, I bring you good tidings of great joy which will be to all people. For there is born to you this day in the city of David a Saviour, who is Christ the Lord. And this will be the sign to you: You will find a Babe wrapped in swaddling cloths, lying in a manger."
And suddenly there was with the angel a multitude of the heavenly host praising God and saying:
"Glory to God in the highest, And on earth peace, goodwill toward men!"

So it was, when the angels had gone away from them into heaven, that the shepherds said to one another,
"Let us now go to Bethlehem and see this thing that has come to pass, which the Lord has made known to us." And they came with haste and found Mary and Joseph, and the Babe lying in a manger. Now when they had seen Him, they made widely known the saying which was told them concerning this Child. And all those who

heard it marvelled at those things which were told them by the shepherds. But Mary kept all these things and pondered them in her heart. Then the shepherds returned, glorifying and praising God for all the things that they had heard and seen, as it was told them.

Imagine the shepherds in their field with their sheep on a dark night.

Picture as far as you can the leading angel and then the angelic host.

Absorb their message to mankind.

Imagine the shepherds hurrying to Bethlehem, perhaps with their crooks in their hands.

Picture the scene in the stable.

Picture Mary and Joseph and the baby Jesus.
Worship with the shepherds, this marvellous and wondrous work of God.

Hymn:

While Shepherds watched their flocks by night,
All seated on the ground,
The angel of the Lord came down,
And glory shone around.

"Fear not," said he for mighty dread
Had seized their troubled mind,
"Great tidings of great joy I bring
To you and all mankind.

To you in David's town this day
Is born of David's line
A Saviour, who is Christ the Lord;
And this shall be the sign:

"The heavenly Babe you there shall find
To human view displayed,
All meanly wrapped in swathing bands,
And in a manger laid."

Thus spake the Seraph; and forthwith
Appeared a shining throng
Of angels praising God, who thus
Addressed their joyful song.

"All glory be to God on high,
And to the earth be peace;
Goodwill hence forth from heav'n to men,
Begin and never cease."[29]

Prayer:

Praise God for the wonder of the Christmas story and the gift of His Son.

Receive and thank God for His priceless gift that has no boundaries and is given to all; for the rich and poor, for the young and old, for the great and small.

Meditation 16: Birth of Jesus from St Matthew's Gospel

Matthew Chapter 1: 18-25

'Now the birth of Jesus Christ was as follows: After His mother Mary was betrothed to Joseph, before they came together, she was found with child of the Holy Spirit. Then Joseph her husband, being a just man, and not wanting to make her a public example, was minded to put her away secretly. But while he thought about these things, behold, an angel of the Lord appeared to him in a dream, saying, "Joseph, son of David, do not be afraid to take to you Mary your wife, for that which is conceived in her is of the Holy Spirit. And she will bring forth a Son, and you shall call His name JESUS, for He will save His people from their sins."

So all this was done that it might be fulfilled which was spoken by the Lord through the prophet, saying:
"Behold, the virgin shall be with child, and bear a Son, and they shall call His name Immanuel," which translated, "God with us."

Then Joseph, being aroused from sleep, did as the angel of the Lord commanded him and took to him his wife, and did not know her till she had brought forth her firstborn Son. And he called His name JESUS.'

'Now after Jesus was born in Bethlehem of Judea in the days of Herod the king, behold, wise men from the East came to Jerusalem, saying, "Where is He who has been born King of the Jews? For we have seen His star in the East and have come to worship Him."
When Herod the king heard this, he was troubled, and all Jerusalem with him. And when he had gathered all the chief priests and scribes of the people together, he inquired of them where the Christ was to be born. So they said to him, "In Bethlehem of Judea, for thus it is written by the prophet: 'But you, Bethlehem, in the land of Judah, are not the least among the rulers of Judah; for out of you shall come a Ruler who will shepherd My people Israel.'"

Then Herod, when he had secretly called the wise men, determined from them what time the star appeared. And he sent them to Bethlehem and said, "Go and search carefully for the young Child, and when you have found Him bring back word to me, that I may come and worship Him also."
When they heard the king, they departed; and behold, the star which they had seen in the East went before them, till it came and stood over where the young Child was. When they saw the star they rejoiced with exceedingly great joy. And when they had come into the house, they saw the young Child with Mary His mother, and fell down and worshipped Him. And when they

**had opened their treasures, they presented gifts to Him: gold, frankincense, and myrrh.
Then, being divinely warned in a dream that they should not return to Herod, they departed for their own country another way.'**

In church liturgy this is called **'The Epiphany',** meaning the manifestation of Jesus to the Gentiles. The three kings were Magi, in other words astrologers.

Picture in your imagination the astrologers (Wise Men) seeing the star in the sky. Imagine the scene in the house (not stable) with the three Wise Men, Joseph and Mary.

See the Wise Men offering their gifts of gold, frankincense, and myrrh. Worship with them the infant Jesus

Colossians Chapter 2: 9

> **'For in Him dwells all the fullness of the God-head bodily; and you are complete in Him, who is the head of all principality and power.'**

Hymn:

> **'Let earth and Heaven combine,
> Angels and men agree,
> To praise in songs divine,
> The incarnate Deity,
> Our God contracted to a span
> Incomprehensibly made man.'**[30]

Hymn:

O worship the Lord in the beauty of holiness,
bow down before Him, his glory proclaim;
with gold of obedience and incense of lowliness,
kneel and adore Him: the Lord is His name.

Low at His feet lay your burden of carefulness,
high on His heart He will bear it for you,
comfort your sorrows, and answer your
prayerfulness,
guiding your steps in the way that is true.

Fear not to enter his courts in the slenderness
Of the poor wealth you would count as your
own;
Truth in its beauty and love in its tenderness,
These are the offerings to bring to His throne.

These, though we bring them in trembling and
fearfulness,
He will accept for the name that is dear;
Mornings of joy give for evenings of tearfulness,
Trust for our trembling, and hope for our fear.

O worship the Lord in the beauty of holiness,
bow down before Him, His glory proclaim;
with gold of obedience and incense of lowliness,
Kneel and adore Him: the Lord is His name.[31]

Prayer:
All I have I give Him, Give Him my heart.

Meditation 17: Jesus' Incarnation

John Chapter 1: 1 - 14

'In the beginning was the Word, and the Word was with God, and the Word was God. He was in the beginning with God. All things were made through Him, and without Him, nothing was made that was made. In Him was life, and the life was the light of men. And the light shines in the darkness, and the darkness did not comprehend it.

There was a man sent from God, whose name was John. This man came for a witness, to bear witness of the Light, that all through Him might believe. He was not that Light, but was sent to bear witness of that Light. That was the true Light which gives light to every man coming into the world. He was in the world, and the world was made through Him, and the world did not know Him. He came to His own, and His own did not receive Him. But as many as received Him, to them He gave the right to become children of God, to those who believe in His name: who were born not of blood, nor of the will of the flesh, nor of the will of man, but of God. And the Word became flesh and dwelt among us, and we beheld His glory, the glory as of the only begotten of the Father, full of grace and truth.'

John speaks about 'The Word'. This certainly means the Lord Jesus Christ, who He describes as the 'Word of God', which means revelation of Himself as the Bible teaches, God was in Christ, and He and the Father are one.

Try to picture in your mind Jesus (God) as a man.

Picture Him in His Rabbinic robes and worship Him in His beauty.

Hymn:

> **O word of God incarnate,**
> **O wisdom from on high,**
> **O Truth unchanged, unchanging,**
> **O Light of our dark sky.**
> **We praise Thee for the radiance**
> **That from the hallowed page,**
> **A lantern to our footsteps,**
> **Shines on from age to age.**[32]

Prayer:

Let all the compassion, purity, and beauty of Jesus be seen in me.
Refine all my nature with Your divine Spirit, so that the radiance of Jesus will shine from me.

Meditation 18: Jesus' Baptism

Luke Chapter 3: 21-22

> **'When all the people were baptized, it came to pass that Jesus also was baptized; and while He prayed, the heaven was opened. And the Holy Spirit descended in bodily form like a dove upon Him, and a voice came from heaven which said, "You are My beloved Son; in You I am well pleased".'**

Imagine the plain covered with grass and then the River Jordan flowing through it.

Picture John the Baptist dressed in camel's hair and a cloth around his waist baptising people by immersion in the river.

Picture Jesus coming to the edge of the river. Picture John baptising Him by immersion. Picture a dove alighting upon Jesus' head. Hear the voice saying, "Thou art my beloved Son in whom I am well pleased."

Recall your own baptism and ask again that you may be filled with the Holy Spirit.

Have you received power for your Christian life and ministry? Are you baptised in the Holy Spirit?

Hymn:

Breathe on me, Breath of God,
Fill me with life anew;
That I may love what Thou dost love,
And do what Thou wouldst do.

Breathe on me, Breath of God,
Until my heart is pure;
Until my will is one with Thine,
To do and to endure.

Breathe on me, Breath of God,
Till I am wholly Thine;
Until this earthly part of me,
Glows with Thy fire divine.

Breathe on me, Breath of God,
So shall I never die,
But live with Thee the perfect life
Of Thine eternity.[33]

Prayer:

God, the Holy Spirit, sovereign, eternal, and divine, I worship and obey You; fill me with Your Breath of Life.

Meditation 19: The Temptations of Jesus Christ by Satan

Luke Chapter 4: 1-13

Then Jesus, being filled with the Holy Spirit, returned from the Jordan and was led by the Spirit into the wilderness, being tempted for forty days by the devil. And in those days He ate nothing, and afterward, when they had ended, He was hungry. And the devil said to Him, "If You are the Son of God, command this stone to become bread." But Jesus answered him, saying, "It is written, 'Man shall not live by bread alone, but by every word of God'."

Then the devil, taking Him up on a high mountain, showed Him all the kingdoms of the world in a moment of time. And the devil said to Him, "All this authority I will give You, and their glory; for this has been delivered to me, and I give it to whomever I wish. Therefore, if You will worship before me, all will be Yours." And Jesus answered and said to him, "Get behind Me, Satan! For it is written, 'You shall worship the LORD your God, and Him only you shall serve'."

Then he brought Him to Jerusalem, set Him on the pinnacle of the temple, and said to Him, "If You are the Son of God, throw Yourself down from here. For it is written: 'He shall give His angels charge over you, To keep you,' and 'In

their hands they shall bear you up, Lest you dash your foot against a stone'." And Jesus answered and said to him, "It has been said, 'You shall not tempt the LORD your God'." Now when the devil had ended every temptation, he departed from Him until an opportune time."

Imagine a wilderness and see Jesus kneeling to pray to His Father. See the devil coming to Jesus as He is in prayer.

See the stone that Satan held in Jesus' sight and hear the words he said in your mind.

See Jesus on a very high mountain with all the world at His feet and again hear what Satan says.

See Jesus on the pinnacle of the temple and hear again what Satan said.

Notice how Jesus answered him quoting the Word of God.

Prayer:

Saviour Christ, You who became a man; You have been tempted, tested and tried. Come and be with me in Your mercy; remind me of Your words that I may use them as a shield against temptation.

Meditation 20: The Beatitudes

Matthew Chapter 5: 1 – 12

'And seeing the multitudes, He went up on a mountain, and when He was seated His disciples came to Him. Then He opened His mouth and taught them saying:

"Blessed are the poor in spirit, for theirs is the kingdom of heaven,

Blessed are those who mourn, for they shall be comforted.

Blessed are the meek, for they shall inherit the earth.

Blessed are those who hunger and thirst for righteousness, for they shall be filled.

Blessed are the merciful, for they shall obtain mercy.

Blessed are the pure in heart, for they shall see God.

Blessed are the peacemakers, for they shall be called sons of God.

Blessed are those who are persecuted for righteousness' sake, for theirs is the kingdom of heaven.

Blessed are you when they revile and persecute you and say all kinds of evil against you falsely for My sake. Rejoice and be exceedingly glad, for great is your reward in Heaven, for so they persecuted the prophets who were before you."

Reflect on one or more of these innermost dispositions and attitudes in your life. Select one and imagine what it is like for this to be a very real part of your life.

You may go on to others on different days. Really absorb each one into your being.

Hymn:

> **Bless'd are the pure in heart**
> **for they shall see our God;**
> **the secret of the Lord is theirs,**
> **their soul is Christ's abode.**
>
> **The Lord, who left the heavens,**
> **our life and peace to bring,**
> **to dwell in lowliness with men,**
> **their pattern and their King.**
>
> **Still to the lowly soul**
> **He doth Himself impart,**
> **and for His dwelling and His throne**
> **Chooseth the pure in heart.**
>
> **Lord, we Thy presence seek;**
> **may ours this blessing be;**
> **give us a pure and lowly heart,**
> **a temple meet for Thee.**[34]

Prayer:
Ask Jesus to make one particular Beatitude (the Greek word meaning blessing) in your heart.

Meditation 21: The Call of the Disciples

Mark Chapter 1: 16-18

> **'And as He walked by the Sea of Galilee, He saw Simon and Andrew his brother casting a net into the sea; for they were fishermen. Then Jesus said to them, "Follow Me, and I will make you become fishers of men."**
> **They immediately left their nets and followed Him.'**

Imagine the scene, the fishing boats moored up to the shore.

See Peter, Andrew, James, and John washing their nets. See Jesus approaching them.

Hear Jesus speaking to them. See the miraculous catch of fish.

Hear Jesus calling them to follow Him.

See them letting go their nets, standing up and following behind Jesus.

Hymn:

> **Jesus calls us o'er the tumult**
> **of our life's wild, restless sea;**
> **day by day His sweet voice soundeth,**
> **saying, "Christian, follow me."**
>
> **As of old, apostles heard it**
> **by the Galilean lake,**
> **turned from home and toil and kindred,**
> **leaving all for His dear sake.**
>
> **Jesus calls us from the worship**
> **of the vain world's golden store,**
> **from each idol that would keep us,**
> **saying, "Christian, love me more."**
>
> **In our joys and in our sorrows,**
> **days of toil and hours of ease,**
> **still He calls, in cares and pleasures,**
> **"Christian, love me more than these."**
>
> **Jesus calls us; by Thy mercies,**
> **Saviour, may we hear Thy call,**
> **give our hearts to thine obedience,**
> **serve and love Thee best of all.**[35]

Prayer:

'O Jesus I have promised to serve Thee to the end.'[36]

Renew this act of consecration and confess anywhere you have failed since you first made this promise.

Meditation 22: The Scope of the Ministry of Jesus

Luke Chapter 4: 16 - 21

> **'So He came to Nazareth, where he had been brought up. And as His custom was, He went into the synagogue on the Sabbath day, and stood up to read. And he was handed the book of the prophet Isaiah. And when He had opened the book, He found the place where it was written: 'The Spirit of the LORD is upon Me, because He has anointed Me to preach the Gospel to the poor; He has sent me to heal the broken hearted, to proclaim liberty to the captives and recovery of sight to the blind, to set at liberty those who are oppressed; to proclaim the acceptable year of the LORD.' Then He closed the book and gave it back to the attendant and sat down. And the eyes of all who were in the synagogue were fixed on Him. And He began to say to them, "Today this scripture is fulfilled in your hearing".'**

This was what Jesus set out to do to fulfil His mission to humanity. Imagine each condition and feel it in a way as your own, for example the poor, the bruised, the prisoners and the blind.

Imagine Jesus ministering to each, and every condition with wonderful healing as a result.

Further reflection: Hebrews Chapter 13: 8

> **'Jesus Christ is the same yesterday, today, and forever.'**

Hymn:

How sweet the name of Jesus sounds
In a believer's ear!
It soothes our sorrows, heals our wounds,
And drives away our fear.

It makes the wounded spirit whole
And calms the troubled breast;
'Tis manna to the hungry soul,
And to the weary, rest.

Jesus, my Shepherd, Saviour, Friend,
My Prophet, Priest and King,
My Lord, my Life, my Way, my End,
Accept the praise I bring.

Weak is the effort of my heart,
And cold my warmest thought;
But when I see You as You are,
I'll praise You as I ought.

Till then I would Your love proclaim
With every fleeting breath;
And may the music of Your Name
Refresh my soul in death.[37]

Prayer:
Pray for yourself if you are in any of the conditions described, and feel the risen Christ ministering to you. Pray also, for anyone you know who would be described in this way and pray for them to be healed or set free by the risen Christ.

Meditation 23: Water into Wine

John Chapter 2: 1 - 10

'On the third day there was a wedding in Cana of Galilee, and the mother of Jesus was there. Now both Jesus and His disciples were invited to the wedding. And when they ran out of wine, the mother of Jesus said to Him, "They have no wine." Jesus said to her, "Woman, what does your concern have to do with Me? My hour has not yet come." His mother said to the servants, "Whatever he says to you, do it."
Now there were set there six waterpots of stone, according to the manner of purification of the Jews, containing twenty or thirty gallons apiece. Jesus said to them, "Fill the waterpots with water." And they filled them up to the brim. And He said to them, "Draw some out now, and take it to the master of the feast." And they took it. When the master of the feast had tasted the water that was made wine, and did not know where it came from (but the servants who had drawn the water knew), the master of the feast called the bridegroom. And he said to him, "Every man at the beginning sets out the good wine, and when the guests have well drunk, then the inferior. You have kept the good wine until now!"

Imagine the scene. At that time weddings went on for about three days. Picture Jesus and the disciples there with Mary His mother.

Enter as far as you can into the festivities which usually involve people getting drunk. Imagine the crisis when the best man finds the wine has run out as this was a very serious event to happen at a wedding feast. Imagine the alarm of the best man telling the bridegroom about the situation. Picture Mary and hear her saying "Whatever He says to you do it."

Imagine the disbelief and the alarm at the servants being told to fill the water bottles with water. These would have been large earthenware vessels, and they were filled to the brim.

Imagine the servants carrying water into the wedding feast with consternation. Then imagine the liquid being tried by the best man and finding it to be the best wine he had ever tasted!

This is called a 'sign' by John, meaning an attesting miracle indicating the divinity and Messiahship of the Lord Jesus. This is really about the transforming presence of Jesus. The other things he transformed: sickness into health, even a cross, a place of defeat, transformed into the means of Salvation; a tomb where dead were laid transformed into a place of resurrection.

Reflect on anything in your life and experience where you have seen the transforming presence of Jesus still at work.

Hymn:

What a wonderful change in my life has been wrought
Since Jesus came into my heart!
I have light in my soul for which long I had sought,
Since Jesus came into my heart!

> **Refrain:**
> **Since Jesus, came into my heart!**
> **Since Jesus came into my heart!**
> **Floods of joy o'er my soul, like the sea billows roll,**
> **Since Jesus came into my heart!**

I have ceased from my wandering and going astray,
Since Jesus came into my heart!
And my sins which were many are all washed away,
Since Jesus came into my heart!

I'm possessed of a hope that is steadfast and sure,
Since Jesus came into my heart!
And no dark clouds of doubt now my pathway obscure,
Since Jesus came into my heart!

There's a light in the valley of death now for me,
Since Jesus came into my heart!
And the gates of the city beyond I can see,
Since Jesus came into my heart!

I shall go there to dwell in that city I know,
Since Jesus came into my heart!
And I'm happy, so happy as onward I go,
Since Jesus came into my heart![38]

Prayer:

Has the now risen Christ to transform anything in your life or circumstances which need such a miraculous act?

Meditation 24: Feeding the Five Thousand

John Chapter 6: 1-14

'After these things Jesus went over the Sea of Galilee, which is the Sea of Tiberias. Then a great multitude followed Him, because they saw His signs which He performed on those who were diseased. And Jesus went up on the mountain, and there He sat with His disciples. Now the Passover, a feast of the Jews, was near.

Then Jesus lifted up His eyes, and seeing a great multitude coming toward Him, He said to Philip, "Where shall we buy bread, that these may eat?" But this He said to test him, for He Himself knew what He would do. Philip answered Him, "Two hundred denarii worth of bread is not sufficient for them, that every one of them may have a little." One of His disciples, Andrew, Simon Peter's brother, said to Him, "There is a lad here who has five barley loaves and two small fish, but what are they among so many?"

Then Jesus said, "Make the people sit down." Now there was much grass in the place. So the men sat down, in number about five thousand. And Jesus took the loaves, and when He had given thanks He distributed them to the disciples, and the disciples to those sitting down; and likewise of the fish, as much as they

wanted. So when they were filled, He said to His disciples, "Gather up the fragments that remain, so that nothing is lost." Therefore they gathered them up, and filled twelve baskets with the fragments of the five barley loaves which were left over by those who had eaten. Then those men, when they had seen the sign that Jesus did, said, "This is truly the Prophet who is to come into the world."

Enter with your imagination into the whole scene, for example, seeing that there was much grass in the place.

Picture the number of people in the crowd, five thousand men, beside women and children, it was indeed a vast crowd for those days.

Hear Jesus bidding them to sit down and see them seated on the grass.

Hear the disciples' consternation, telling Jesus about the fact they needed some food. See a boy handing the disciples five barley loaves and two fish and hear them say "What are they among so many people.?"

See Jesus taking them and blessing them and handing them back to the disciples. See them feeding every person to the full. Importantly, see they were multiplied as they were given away.

Reflect on the concluding verses and marvel at the way Jesus multiplies even the small things we can offer Him.

For further reflection: John Chapter 6: 35

'And Jesus said to them, "I am the Bread of Life. He who comes to Me shall never hunger, and he who believes in Me shall never thirst."

John Chapter 6: 53-58

'Then Jesus said to them, "Most assuredly, I say to you, unless you eat the flesh of the Son of Man and drink His blood, you have no life in you. Whoever eats My flesh and drinks My blood has eternal life, and I will raise him up at the last day. For My flesh is food indeed, and My blood is drink indeed. He who eats My flesh and drinks My blood abides in Me, and I in him.

As the living Father sent Me, and I live because of the Father, so he who feeds on Me will live because of Me. This is the bread which came down from heaven - not as your fathers ate the manna and are dead. He who eats this bread will live forever."

Hymn:

Break thou the Bread of Life, dear Lord, to me,
As Thou did break the loaves beside the sea.
Beyond the sacred page I seek Thee, Lord;
My spirit pants for Thee, O living Word!

Bless Thou the truth, dear Lord, to me, to me,
As Thou didst bless the bread by Galilee.
Then shall all bondage cease, all fetters fall;
And I shall find my peace, my all in all.

Thou art the bread of life, dear Lord, to me,
Thy holy Word the truth that saveth me.
Give me to eat and live with Thee above;
Teach me to love Thy truth, for Thou art love.

Oh, send Thy Spirit now, dear Lord, to me,
That He may touch my eyes, and make me see:
Show me the truth concealed within Thy Word,
for in Thy Book revealed I see Thee Lord.[39]

Prayer:
Thank God for His provision for our material needs. Offer to Him all you can give to Him, as I, in a way, have offered this book, a small offering, and ask Him by His Grace to multiply His blessings upon the readers.

Finish with a prayer of consecration, giving your life into the hands of Jesus.

Meditation 25: The Houses Built on Rock and Sand

Matthew Chapter 7: 24-28

'Therefore whoever hears these saying of Mine, and does them, I will liken him to a wise man who built his house on the rock: and then rain descended, the floods came, and the winds blew and beat on that house; and it did not fall, for it was founded on the rock. But everyone who hears these sayings of Mine, and does not do them, will be like a foolish man who built his house on the sand: and the rain descended, the floods came, and the winds blew and beat on that house; and it fell. And great was its fall.

And so it was, when Jesus had ended these sayings, that the people were astonished at His teaching, for He taught them as one having authority, and not as the scribes.'

Picture these two houses; see the tremendous storm blowing upon each one.

See one totally collapse to the ground and the other standing impregnable on a rock.

Reflect on what the difference is between the two houses. Jesus talked about us keeping His commandments.
For further reflection: 1 Samuel 1

For further reflection: 1 Samuel Chapter 15:22

'Behold, to obey is better than sacrifice, and to heed than the fat of rams.'

Hymn:

O safe the Rock which is higher than I,
My soul in its conflicts and sorrows would fly.
So sinful, so weary, Thine, Thine would I be;
Thou blest Rock of Ages I'm hiding in Thee

> **Refrain:**
> **Hiding in Thee, hiding in Thee,**
> **Thou blest Rock of Ages, I'm hiding in**
> **Thee.**

In the calm of the noontide, in sorrow's lone hour,
In times when temptation casts o'er me its power,
In the tempests of life, on its wide, heaving sea,
Thou blest Rock of Ages, I'm hiding in Thee.

How oft in the conflict, when pressed by the foe,
I have fled to my Refuge and breathed out my woe.
How often when trials like sea-billows roll
Have I hidden in Thee, O Rock of my soul.[40]

Prayer:
Thank God for seeing you through any storms of life you and your family have been through and put your trust in God to guide you to his safe haven – Heaven.

Meditation 26: The Storm on the Sea of Galilee

Mark Chapter 4: 35-41

'On the same day, when evening had come, He said to them, "Let us cross over to the other side." Now when they had left the multitude, they took Him along in the boat as He was. And other little boats were also with Him. And a great windstorm arose, and the waves beat into the boat, so that it was already filling. But He was in the stern, asleep on a pillow. And they awoke Him and said to Him, "Teacher, do You not care that we are perishing?"
Then He arose and rebuked the wind, and said to the sea, "Peace, be still!" And the wind ceased and there was a great calm. But He said to them, "Why are you so fearful? How is it that you have no faith?" And they feared exceedingly, and said to one another, "Who can this be, that even the wind and the sea obey Him!"

See the disciples setting out on the Sea of Galilee on a very lovely, calm evening.

See and hear the terrible storm that suddenly arose, as it often does on the Sea of Galilee. See Jesus fast asleep on a pillow in the stern of the boat, not even awakened by the noise of the storm.

See the panic of the disciples as they tried to bail out the sea from the boat, probably using buckets. See the boat beginning to sink. Hear the panic-stricken call of the disciples "Master don't you care that we perish?"

See Jesus slowly stand up. Hear Him rebuke the disciples for their lack of faith. Hear Him loudly command the storm to cease. See everything becoming a great calm.

Have you sometimes wanted to cry out "Master, don't you care that I perish amid the storms of life?" because of massive events overwhelming you. Consider that Jesus could sleep through this because He knew everything was under control. Wonder at the words "Who can this be that even the wind and the waves obey Him?" Have you faith like this; that no matter what is happening, Jesus is in control of the situation?

Hymn:

> **Jesus lover of my soul, let me to Thy bosom fly,**
> **While the nearer waters roll, while the tempest still is high.**
> **Guard me, O my Saviour, guard, till the storm of life be past;**
> **safe into Thy haven guide, O receive my soul at last.** [41]

Prayer:
Confess any time you have lacked faith when troubles have come, and renew your faith in the Lord Jesus Christ, to be the Lord of your life.

Meditation 27: Jesus the Healer

Mark Chapter 1: 32 - 34

'At evening, when the sun had set, they brought to Him all who were sick and those who were demon-possessed. And the whole city was gathered together at the door. Then He healed many who were sick with various diseases, and cast out many demons; and He did not allow the demons to speak, because they knew Him.'

Luke Chapter 6: 17 - 19

'And He came down with them and stood on a level place with a crowd of His disciples and a great multitude of people from all Judea and Jerusalem, and from the seacoast of Tyre and Sidon, who came to hear Him and be healed of their diseases, as well as those who were tormented with unclean spirits. And they were healed. And the whole multitude sought to touch Him, for power went out from Him and healed them all.'

Hebrews Chapter 13: 8

'Jesus Christ is the same yesterday, today, and forever.'

The accounts of Jesus healing the sick and infirm is on nearly every page of the Gospel. There are forty-one accounts.

Here are some of the well-known accounts, try to imagine the impact on the individuals and their families and neighbours:

        Peter's mother-in-law
        The leper
        The withered hand
        Jairus' daughter
        The deaf and dumb
        The blind
        The man with dropsy
        Lazarus

Meditate on the compassion of Jesus seen in these healings of sick people.

Imagine the scene when the sun was setting; all these sick people, a great crowd of them, gathering together, sitting on the ground. They had heard of Jesus' amazing healing power and came hoping He would heal them.

See Jesus approaching this great crowd, laying His hands on sick people and healing them all indiscriminately.

Think of the amazing energy and power He must have had to accomplish healing all these sick people.

Hymn:

At even, ere the sun was set,
The sick, O Lord, around Thee lay;
O in what divers pains they met!
O with what joy they went away!

Once more 'tis eventide, and we
Oppressed with various ills draw near;
What if Thy form we cannot see?
We know and feel that Thou are here.

O Saviour Christ, our woes dispel;
For some are sick, and some are sad;
And some have never loved Thee well,
And some have lost the love they had;

And some have found the world in vain,
Yet from the world they break not free;
And some have friends who give them pain,
Yet have not sought a friend in Thee;

And none, O Lord, have perfect rest,
For none are wholly free from sin;
And they who fain would serve Thee best
Are conscious most of wrong within.

O Saviour Christ, Thou too art man;
Thou hast been troubled, tempted, tried;
Thy kind but searching glance can scan
The very wounds that shame would hide.

Thy touch has still its ancient power;
No word from Thee can fruitless fall;
Hear, in this solemn evening hour,
And in Thy mercy heal us all.[42]

Prayer:

Pray about any sickness or infirmity you may have, and any people known to you who are afflicted like this and pray that Jesus will indeed heal them as they seek His presence and feel His touch, either suddenly or gradually, and that they will give Jesus the glory due to Him.

Meditation 28: Jesus the Deliverer

Mark Chapter 1:21- 27

> **Then they went into Capernaum, and immediately on the Sabbath He entered the synagogue and taught. And they were astonished at His teaching, for He taught them as one having authority, and not as the scribes. Now there was a man in their synagogue with an unclean spirit. And He cried out saying, "Let us alone! What have we to do with You, Jesus of Nazareth? Did You come to destroy? I know who You are - the Holy One of God!"**
>
> **But Jesus rebuked him saying, "Be quiet, and come out of him!". And when the unclean spirit had convulsed him and cried out with a loud voice, he came out of him. Then they were all amazed, so that they questioned among themselves, saying, "What is this? What new doctrine is this? For with authority He commands even the unclean spirits, and they obey Him."**

Consider the wonderful, and always victorious, power Jesus had over all the forces of evil in peoples' lives.

With authority He casts out the demons and they obey Him.

Hymn:

And can it be that I should gain
An interest in the Saviour's blood?
Died He for me, who caused His pain?
For me, who Him to death pursued?
Amazing love! How can it be,
That Thou, my God, shouldst die for Me?
Amazing love! How can it be,
That Thou, my God, shouldst die for me?

He left His Father's throne above,
So free, so infinite His grace;
Emptied Himself of all but love,
And bled for Adam's helpless race:
'Tis mercy all, immense and free,
For, O my God, it found out me!
'Tis mercy all, immense and free,
For, O my God, it found out me!

Long my imprisoned spirit lay,
Fast bound in sin and nature's night;
Thine eye diffused a quick'ning ray,
I woke, the dungeon flamed with light;
My chains fell off, my heart was free,
I rose, went forth, and followed Thee.
My chains fell off, my heart was free,
I rose, went forth, and followed Thee.[43]

Prayer:
Pray for any you know who are in any kind of bondage to fear, or depression, alcohol, or drugs. Pray for any person you know who is in prison and pray for the Christian work that goes on in many prisons. Pray for drug rehabilitation centres and all such related Christian Ministries.

Meditation 29: The Parable of the Sower

Mark Chapter 4: 2-20

Then He taught them many things by parables, and said to them in His teaching: "Listen! Behold, a sower went out to sow. And it happened, as he sowed, that some seed fell by the wayside; and the birds of the air came and devoured it. Some fell on stony ground, where it did not have much earth; and immediately it sprang up because it had no depth of earth. But when the sun was up it was scorched, and because it had no root it withered away. And some seed fell among thorns; and the thorns grew up and choked it, and it yielded no crop. But other seed fell on good ground and yielded a crop that sprang up, increased and produced: some thirtyfold, some sixty, and some a hundred." And He said to them, "He who has ears to hear, let them hear!"

But when He was alone, those around Him with the twelve asked Him about the parable. And He said to them, "To you it has been given to know the mystery of the kingdom of God; but to those who are outside, all things come in parables, so that 'Seeing they may see and not perceive, and hearing they may hear and not understand; lest they should turn, and their sins be forgiven them.'"

And He said to them, "Do you not understand this parable? How then will you understand all the parables? The sower sows the word. And these are the ones by the wayside where the word is sown. When they hear, Satan comes immediately and takes away the word that was sown in their hearts. These likewise are the ones sown on stony ground who, when they hear the word, immediately receive it with gladness; and they have no root in themselves, and so endure only for a time. Afterward, when tribulation or persecution arises for the word's sake, immediately they stumble. Now these are the ones sown among the thorns; they are the ones who hear the word, and the cares of this world, the deceitfulness of riches, and the desires for other things entering in choke the word, and it becomes unfruitful. But these are the ones sown on good ground, those who hear the word, accept it, and bear fruit: some thirtyfold, some sixty, and some a hundred."

Picture the sower walking slowly through the field with a basket of seed under his left arm, putting his right hand in the basket and flinging the seed to the right and left indiscriminately.

Picture the different types of soil in which the seed is falling as in the parable.

Has the seed of the Gospel fallen on good soil in your life?

Remember the words of Paul,

'I planted, Apollos watered, but God gave the increase.' [44]

Remember also the words of Jesus to His disciples,

"The harvest is truly plentiful, but the labourers are few. Therefore, pray the Lord of the harvest to send out labourers into His harvest." [45]

Hymn:

**We plough the field and scatter
the good seed on the land,
But it is fed and watered by
God's almighty hand:
He sends the snow in winter,
the warmth to swell the grain,
The breezes and the sunshine,
and soft refreshing rain.
All good gifts around us are sent from heaven above;
Then thank the Lord, O thank the Lord for all His love.**

**He only is the Maker
of all things near and far;
He paints the wayside flower,
He lights the evening star;**

The winds and waves obey Him,
by Him the birds are fed;
Much more to us, His children,
He gives our daily bread.
All good gifts around us are sent from heaven
above,
Then thank the Lord, O thank the Lord for all His
love.

We thank Thee, then, O Father,
for all things bright and good,
The seed time and the harvest,
our life, our health, our food;
No gifts we have to offer
for all Thy love imparts;
But that which Thou desirest,
our humble, thankful, hearts.
All good gifts around us are sent from heaven
above,
Then thank the Lord, O thank the Lord for all His
love.[46]

Reflect on the opening line of the hymn and for the word 'land' substitute 'human heart'.

Prayer:

Picture this as the seed of the apostles being scattered.
Pray for revival.

Meditation 30: The Prodigal Son

Luke Chapter 15: 11-31

Then He said, "A certain man had two sons. And the younger of them said to his father, 'Father, give me the portion of goods that falls to me.' So he divided to them his livelihood. And not many days after, the younger son gathered all together, journeyed to a far country, and there wasted his possessions with prodigal living.

But when he had spent all, there arose a severe famine in that land, and he began to be in want. Then he went and joined himself to a citizen of that country, and he sent him into his fields to feed swine. And he would gladly have filled his stomach with the pods that the swine ate, and no one gave him anything. But when he came to himself, he said, 'How many of my father's hired servants have bread enough and to spare, and I perish with hunger! I will arise and go to my father, and will say to him, "Father, I have sinned against heaven and before you, and I am no longer worthy to be called your son. Make me like one of your hired servants".'

And he arose and came to his father. But when he was still a great way off, his father saw him and had compassion, and ran and fell on his neck and kissed him. And the son said to him, "Father, I have sinned against heaven and in your sight, and am no longer worthy to be called your son.' But the father said to his servants, 'Bring out the best robe and put it on him, and put a ring on his hand and sandals on his feet. And bring the fatted calf here and kill it, and let us eat and be merry; for this my son was dead and is alive again; he was lost and is found.' And they began to be merry.

Now his older son was in the field. And as he came and drew near to the house, he heard music and dancing. So he called one of the servants and asked what these things meant. And he said to him, 'Your brother has come, and because he has received him safe and sound, your father has killed the fatted calf.' But he was angry and would not go in. Therefore his father came out and pleaded with him. So he answered and said to his father, 'Lo, these many years I have been serving you; I never transgressed your commandment at any time; and yet you never game me a young goat, that I may make merry with my friends. But as soon as this son of yours came, who has devoured your livelihood with harlots, you killed the fatted calf for him.' And he said to him, 'Son, you are always with me, and all that I have is yours. It was right that we should make merry and be glad, for your brother was dead and is alive again, and was lost and is found.'

Notice the wonderful relationship between the father and his sons, typifying God's relationship with us.

Notice the son's free will, even to leave home. So we have free will to leave our relationship with the heavenly father, as it were, to spend our spiritual inheritance. Notice how terribly deep this son's fall was because, to Jews, a swine was the utmost unclean beast.

Reflect on your free will; how anyone can become a 'backslider', far away from God, and notice that coming home is called 'coming to our senses'.

Notice that the father went out every day scouring the horizon in case his son was coming home. This again is God's relationship with those who have gone away from Him.

Notice how the son is rapidly restored to his status. He could not be made a servant because he had the blood of the son of the father in his veins.

Notice the father's loving restoration of the status of his son, who he later describes as 'was lost and is found again', 'was dead and is alive again'. Such is God's restoration of anyone lost, no matter how reckless they have been in their living. This restoration can be described as 'coming home'.

Reflect on the attitude of the other brother and whether it is possible for long-serving Christians ever to resent such a joyous welcome for someone who has fallen deeply into sin and yet may receive from God his restoration.

If you read the rest of this chapter you will see the joy of the lost being found, a coin and a sheep.

Know there is joy in the presence of God, as stated by Jesus, 'over one sinner that repents'.

Hymn:

> **I've wandered far away from God,**
> **And now I am coming home;**
> **The paths of sin too long I've trod,**
> **Lord, I'm coming home.**
>
> **Coming home, coming home,**
> **Nevermore to roam,**
> **Open wide Thine arms of love,**
> **Lord, I'm coming home.**[47]

It has been my joy as a world-wide evangelist to see such homecomings happen very frequently.

Prayer:
Thank God if you have ever been lost and have now come home.
Pray for any you know who are lost, remembering,

> **Jesus is seeking the wanderers yet; why do they roam?**
> **Love only waits to forgive and forget; home weary wanderer, home.**
> **Wonderful love dwells in the heart of the Father above.**[48]

Meditation 31: The Good Samaritan

Luke Chapter 10: 25-37

And behold, a certain lawyer stood up and tested Him saying, "Teacher, what shall I do to inherit eternal life?" He said to him, "What is written in the law? What is your reading of it?" So he answered and said, "You shall love the LORD your God with all your heart, with all your soul, with all your strength, and with all your mind, and your neighbour as yourself." And He said to him, "You have answered rightly; do this and you will live." But he, wanting to justify himself, said to Jesus, "And who is my neighbour?"

Then Jesus answered and said: "A certain man went down from Jerusalem to Jericho, and fell among thieves, who stripped him of his clothing, wounded him, and departed, leaving him half dead. Now by chance a certain priest came down that road. And when he saw him, he passed by on the other side. Likewise a Levite, when he arrived at the place, came and looked, and passed by on the other side. But a certain Samaritan, as he journeyed, came where he was. And when he saw him, he had compassion. So he went to him and bandaged his wounds, pouring on oil and wine; and he set him on his own animal, brought him to an inn, and took care of him. On the next day, when he departed, he took out two denarii, gave them to the

innkeeper, and said to him, 'Take care of him; and whatever more you spend, when I come again I will repay you.' So which of these three do you think was neighbour to him who fell among the thieves?" And he said, "He who showed mercy on him." Then Jesus said to him, "Go and do likewise."

Reflect deeply on the first and greatest commandment which Jesus enumerated: You shall love the Lord your God with all your heart, this means with all your emotions; your soul equals all your spiritual life; your strength is all your will; your mind is all your thinking, reasoning, and intellectual capacity. This means loving the Lord with all your being.

You shall love your neighbour as yourself - the second commandment, we must see is not love your neighbour and not yourself but love your neighbour _as_ yourself. This means an outgoing love to other people when we have the right self-love.

Reflect on all this and what it means for you.

In answer to the question 'Who is my neighbour?' Jesus posits the parable of the Good Samaritan. This is a time for using your imagination and entering into the whole scene of a very long road going from Jerusalem to Jericho. This road was well-known to be inhabited by thieves and robbers.

Picture the Jewish man going along the road. Picture robbers leaping out from behind rocks. See them beating the man mercilessly and robbing him of all that he has.

See the priest and the Levite ignoring the helpless man who was half dead. It was not their business, they had not beaten the man and thought they had more important things to do.

See the man who Jesus says was a Samaritan crossing all the known bounds of racial behaviour between Samaritans and Jews and going to the help of the stricken Jewish man.

See him 'pouring on oil and wine', very important medicants at that time.

See him setting him on his own ass and taking him to an inn, a place of safety. Hear the Samaritan leaving this Jew in a safe place and stating that he would give the whole cost of what the Jewish man's care would be.

Notice that Jesus turns this question about 'Who is my neighbour' completely around. Are you neighbourly?

Reflect on your own life, especially in respect of any kind of racial or cultural dislike or even hatred you may feel, not just to people of another colour or nationality but even very poor people, even scroungers.

Hymn:

O Thou Who camest from above
The pure celestial fire to impart,
Kindle a flame of sacred love
On the mean altar of my heart.

There let it for Thy glory burn
With inextinguishable blaze,
And trembling to its source return
In humble prayer and fervent praise

Jesus, confirm my heart's desire
To work, and speak, and think for Thee;
Still let me guard the holy fire,
And still stir up Thy gift in me.

Ready for all Thy perfect will,
My acts of faith and love repeat,
Till death Thy endless mercies seal,
And make the sacrifice complete.[49]

Prayer:

Confess any failings you need to bring to the Lord.

Ask God to help you to see how you can always be a neighbourly person, especially helping those in physical need, even giving financially to the poor.

Meditation 32: The Transfiguration

Matthew Chapter 17: 1-13

Now after six days Jesus took Peter, James, and John his brother, led them up on a high mountain by themselves; and He was transfigured before them. His face shone like the sun, and His clothes became as white as the light. And behold, Moses and Elijah appeared to them, talking with Him. Then Peter answered and said to Jesus, "Lord, it is good for us to be here; if You wish, let us make here three tabernacles: one for You, one for Moses, and one for Elijah." While he was still speaking, behold, a bright cloud overshadowed them; and suddenly a voice came out of the cloud, saying, "This is My beloved Son, in whom I am well pleased. Hear Him!" And when the disciples heard it, they fell on their faces and were greatly afraid. But Jesus came and touched them and said, "Arise, and do not be afraid." When they had lifted up their eyes, they saw no one but Jesus only.

Now as they came down from the mountain, Jesus commanded them, saying, "Tell the vision to no one until the Son of Man is risen from the dead." And His disciples asked Him, saying, "Why then do the scribes say that Elijah must come first?" Jesus answered and said to them, "Indeed, Elijah is coming first and will restore all things. But I say to you that Elijah has come

already, and they did not know him but did to him whatever they wished. Likewise the Son of Man is also about to suffer at their hands." Then the disciples understood that He spoke to them of John the Baptist.

2 Corinthians Chapter 5: 18 - 19

Now all things are of God, who has reconciled us to Himself through Jesus Christ, and has given us the ministry of reconciliation, that is, that God was in Christ reconciling the world to Himself, not imputing their trespasses to them, and has committed to us the word of reconciliation.

Picture this wonderful scene on a mountain with Peter, James, and John, seeing the glory of Jesus in an ethereal manner - a picture of His true self.

The presence of Moses and Elijah from their heavenly rest, signifies that Jesus fulfilled the Law of Moses and the Prophets.

Enter into the confusion of the disciples and hear Jesus' words to them.

Hear the voice saying, 'This is My beloved Son, in Whom I am well pleased. Hear Him!'

Hymn:

Eternal light, eternal light!
How pure the soul must be
When, placed within your searching sight,
It does not fear, but with delight
Can face such majesty.

The spirits who surround your throne
May bear that burning bliss;
But that is surely theirs alone,
Since they have never, never known
A fallen world like this.

O how shall I whose dwelling here
Is dark, whose mind is dim,
Before a holy God appear
And on my naked spirit bear
The uncreated beam?

There is a way for us to rise
To that sublime abode:
An offering and a sacrifice,
A Holy Spirit's energies
An advocate with God.

Such grace prepares us for the sight
of holiness above;
The child of ignorance and night
May dwell in the eternal light
Through the eternal love.[50]

Prayer:

Worship Jesus, especially His divine presence still in the world.

Pray that you will have a similar vision that graphically speaks to you of the coming of God's kingdom, a kingdom of power.

Pray that all who need to will see His wonderful being and give their lives to Him.

Meditation 33: Jesus the Giver of Rest

Matthew Chapter 11: 28-30

> "Come to Me, all you who labour and are heavy laden, and I will give you rest. Take My yoke upon you and learn from Me, for I am gentle and lowly in heart, and you find rest for your souls. For My yoke is easy and My burden is light."

Hebrews Chapter 4:1-3

> 'Therefore, since a promise remains of entering His rest, let us fear lest any of you seem to have come short of it. For indeed the gospel was preached to us as well as to them; but the word which they heard did not profit them, not being mixed with faith in those who heard it. For we who have believed do enter that rest.'

Picture a yoke of oxen striving to climb a very steep hill pulling a very heavy load in the cart behind them. This is what life can be like in picture form without Jesus.

Hear His wonderful invitation for all who are struggling and the promise that those who exchange the yoke of oxen for His yoke in life's struggle, will find that following Him is wonderful ease and rest. The Christian life is not difficult.

Hymn:

> **There is a place of quiet and rest,**
> **Near to the heart of God,**
> **A place where sin cannot molest,**
> **Near to the heart of God**

>> **Refrain:**
>> **O Jesus, blest Redeemer,**
>> **Sent from the heart of God,**
>> **Hold us, who wait before Thee,**
>> **Near to the heart of God**

> **There is a place of comfort sweet,**
> **Near to the heart of God,**
> **A place where we our Saviour meet,**
> **Near to the heart of God.**

> **There is a place of full release,**
> **Near to the heart of God,**
> **A place where all is joy and peace,**
> **Near to the heart of God.**[51]

Prayer:

Pray that you will hear and respond to Jesus' gracious invitation to rest.

Pray that by laying down your trouble you will cease also to be a source of trouble to others.

Pray for anyone you know that also needs to respond to this wonderful invitation.

Meditation 34: I am the Light of the World

John Chapter 8: 12

> **Then Jesus spoke to them again, saying, "I am the light of the world. He who follows Me shall not walk in darkness, but have the light of life."**

See the world in pitch black darkness, that is its spiritual state now. See every human being without Christ, walking, as it were, like a blind man.

See Jesus Himself as a light, to give meaning and purpose to the whole world, and see every individual, probably even yourself at one time, stumbling through life.

This meditation of Jesus being a great light to show the way of salvation, and the way to the true living God, which, when we have 'seen the light', transforms the meaning and purpose of the whole of our life.

Remember John Chapter 1; 9, where it is said of Jesus

> **'That was the true Light which gives light to every man coming into the world.'**

Hymn:

Thou whose almighty word
Chaos and darkness heard
And took their flight,
Hear us we humbly pray,
And where the gospel day
Sheds not its glorious ray
Let There Be Light!

Saviour who came to give
Those who in darkness live
Healing and sight,
Health to the troubled mind,
Sight to the inward blind,
Now to all humankind
Let There Be Light!

Spirit of truth and love,
Life-giving, holy dove,
Speed forth thy flight;
Move o'er the waters face,
Bearing the lamp of grace
And in earth's darkest place
Let There Be Light![52]

Prayer:
Pray for the spread of the Gospel throughout the world especially in lands where pagan religions flourish e.g. Hinduism and Buddhism. Pray for all missionaries who are working in these lands, especially any you know, and pray for the missionary societies e.g. The Church Missionary Society and the Leprosy Mission and others you may know of who are seeking to spread the gospel in these lands.

Meditation 35: I am the Way, the Truth, and the Life

John Chapter 14: 1 - 6

> "Let not your heart be troubled; you believe in
> God, believe also in Me. In My Father's house
> are many mansions; if it were not so, I would
> have told you. I go to prepare a place for you.
> And if I go to prepare a place for you, I will
> come again and receive you to Myself; that
> where I am, there you may be also. And where I
> go you know, and the way you know."
> Thomas said to Him, "Lord, we do not know
> where You are going, and how can we know the
> way?"
> Jesus said to him, "I am the way, the truth, and
> the life. No one comes to the Father except
> through Me."

You are, as it were, walking through life and feel very lost
on this planet at this time.

There are no signposts indicating which way you must go
and, in fact you do not know where you are going.

However, since you have come to know Jesus personally, as
the way, the truth, and the life, now you know precisely
where you are going and the way to reach your eternal
destination.

Hymn:

Thou art the Way: to Thee alone
From sin and death we flee;
And he who would the Father seek,
Must seek him, Lord by Thee.

Thou art the Truth: Thy Word alone
True wisdom can impart;
Thou only canst inform the mind,
And purify the heart.

Thou art the Life: the rending tomb
Proclaims Thy conquering arm,
And those who put their trust in Thee
Nor death nor hell shall harm.

Thou art the Way, the Truth, the Life:
Grant us that Way to know,
That Truth to keep, that Life to win,
Whose joys eternal flow.[53]

Prayer:

Remember the time when you came to know Jesus in a personal way either as a sudden experience or gradually. Thank Him for His presence with you at every moment in your life, and this all through Grace - God's unending and unmerited love for you. Confess if you have ever strayed from the way and renew your determination to walk with Christ in your heart.

Meditation 36: I am the Resurrection and the Life

John Chapter 11: 25

> Jesus said to her, "I am the resurrection and the life. He who believes in Me, though He may die, he shall live. And whoever lives and believes in Me shall never die. Do you believe this?"

Think of this incredible and fantastic claim Jesus makes about Himself.

Reflect on the fact that He does not say 'anyone who believes in me God will give him eternal life', what He says is that, in Him, in His Person, there is eternal life for all who believe in Him.

Revelation Chapter 1: 18

> "I am He who lives, and was dead, and behold, I am alive forevermore. Amen."

Hymn:

> Forever with the Lord!
> Amen! So let it be.
> Life from the dead is in that word,
> 'Tis immortality.

My Father's house on high,
Home of my soul, how near
At times to faith's foreseeing eye
Thy golden gates appear!

Forever with the Lord!
O Father, 'tis Thy will,
The promise of that faithful word
E'en here to me fulfil.

Be Thou at my right hand,
Then can I never fail,
Uphold Thou me, and I shall stand;
Fight Thou, and I'll prevail.

So when my dying breath
Shall set my spirit free,
By death I shall escape from death
To endless life with Thee.

Knowing as I am known;
How shall I live that word
And of repeat before the throne
"Forever with the Lord!"[54]

Prayer:

Pray for any you know who have been bereaved. And for yourself if you have suffered bereavement, and ask that they, like you, will find all the answers to the mysteries of life and death in the person and relationship with Jesus.

Meditation 37: The Raising of Lazarus

John Chapter 11: 14 - 44

Then Jesus said to them plainly, "Lazarus is dead. And I am glad for your sakes that I was not there, that you may believe. Nevertheless, let us go to him." Then Thomas, who is called the Twin, said to his fellow disciples, "Let us also go, that we might die with Him" So when Jesus came, He found that he had already been in the tomb four days. Now Bethany was near Jerusalem, about two miles away. And many of the Jews had joined the women around Martha and Mary, to comfort them concerning their brother. Then Martha, as soon as she heard that Jesus was coming, went and met Him, but Mary was sitting in the house.

Now Martha said to Jesus, "Lord, if You had been here, my brother would not have died. But even now I know that whatever You ask of God, God will give You." Jesus said to her, "Your brother will rise again."

Martha said to Him, "I know that he will rise again in the resurrection at the last day." Jesus said to her, "I am the resurrection and the life. He who believes in Me, though he may die, he shall live. And whoever lives and believes in Me shall never die. Do you believe this?" She said to Him, "Yes, Lord, I believe that You are the Christ, the Son of God, who is to come into the world."

And when she had said these things, she went her way and secretly called Mary her sister, saying, "The Teacher has come and is calling for you." As soon as she heard that, she arose quickly and came to Him. Now Jesus had not yet come into the town, but was in the place where Martha met Him. Then the Jews who were with her in the house, and comforting her, when they saw that Mary rose up quickly and went out, followed her, saying, "She is going to the tomb to weep there." Then, when Mary came where Jesus was, and saw Him, she fell down at His feet, saying to Him, "Lord, if You had been here, my brother would not have died." Therefore, when Jesus saw her weeping, and the Jews who came with her weeping, He groaned in the spirit and was troubled. And He said, "Where have you laid him?" They said to Him, "Lord, come and see." Jesus wept. Then the Jews said, "See how He loved him!" And some of them said, "Could not this Man, who opened the eyes of the blind, also have kept this man from dying?"

Then Jesus, again, groaning in Himself, came to the tomb. It was a cave, and a stone lay against it. Jesus said, "Take away the stone." Martha, the sister of him who was dead, said to Him, "Lord, by this time there is a stench, for he has been dead four days." Jesus said to her, "Did I not say to you that if you would believe you would see the glory of God?" Then they took away the stone from the place where the dead man was lying. And Jesus lifted up His eyes and said, "Father, I thank you that You have heard Me. And I know that you always hear Me, but because of the people who are standing by I

said this, that they may believe that You sent Me."
Now when He had said these things He cried with a loud voice, "Lazarus, come forth!" And he who had died came out bound hand and foot with grave clothes, and his face was wrapped with a cloth. Jesus said to them, "Loose him, and let him go."

Picture the whole scene, including Mary and Martha weeping; the cave and the stone rolled across the entrance.

See the authority of the Lord Jesus in this situation and His belief in His Father and in Himself to perform the most remarkable miracle He ever did.

Feel the compassion of Jesus for those who were sorrowing. 'Jesus wept' Is the shortest verse in the Bible.

Feel Jesus groaning in agony at the distress of the mourners, but also groaning deeply in Himself preparing for the incredible prayer He was going to offer.

Hear Jesus' word of command, despite their disbelief because Lazarus was suffering from rigor mortis. See Lazarus coming out all bound with grave clothes and hear Jesus' command finishing the whole episode with the words, "Loose him and let him go."

Ponder when Lazarus came forth; he was still bound with grave clothes; when Jesus rose from the dead, he left His grave clothes behind - a complete release.

Hymn:

Jesus shall reign where'er the sun
Does its successive journeys run,
His kingdom stretch from shore to shore,
Till moons shall wax and wane no more

People and realms of every tongue
Dwell on His love with sweetest song,
And infant voices shall proclaim
Their early blessings on His name.

Blessings abound where'er He reigns:
The prisoners leap to lose their chains,
The weary find eternal rest,
And all who suffer want are blest.

Let every creature rise and bring
The highest honours to our King,
Angels descend with songs again,
And earth repeat the loud Amen![55]

Prayer:

Jesus be at my end and at my departing. And in David's words in Psalm 23,

'Yea, though I walk through the valley of the
shadow of death, I will fear no evil; for You are
with me; Your rod and Your staff, they comfort
me.'[56]

Meditation 38: The Triumphal Entry

Luke Chapter 19: 29 - 40

And it came to pass, when He drew near to Bethphage, and Bethany, at the mountain called Olivet, that He sent two of His disciples, saying, "Go into the village opposite you, where as you enter you will find a colt tied, on which no one has ever sat. Loose it and bring it here. And if anyone asks you, 'Why are you loosing it? thus you shall say to him, 'Because the Lord has need of it'." So those who were sent went their way and found it just as He had said to them. But as they were loosing the colt, the owners of it said to them, "Why are you loosing the colt?" And they said, "The Lord has need of him." Then they brought him to Jesus. And they threw their own clothes on the colt, and they set Jesus on him. And as He went, many spread their clothes on the road.

Then, as He was now drawing near the descent of the Mount of Olives, the whole multitude of the disciples began to rejoice and praise God with a loud voice for all the mighty works they had seen, saying: "Blessed is the King who comes in the name of the LORD! Peace in heaven and glory in the highest!" And some of the Pharisees called to Him from the crowd, "Teacher, rebuke Your disciples." But He answered and said to them, "I tell you that if these should keep silent, the stones and would immediately cry out."

Picture the whole scene - Jesus riding on an ass, on a well-known path on Mount Olivet to Jerusalem.

See the crowds decking His way with palm leaves.

Hear the cries of the people praising Jesus and remember the fickleness of the crowd for very soon they would be crying, "Crucify Him! Crucify Him!"

See that Jesus by His action was fulfilling the prophecy of Zechariah and in so doing was proclaiming publicly that He was the Messiah whom they were expecting to come and release them from Roman rule.

> **'Rejoice greatly, O daughter of Zion! Shout, O daughter of Jerusalem! Behold, your King is coming to you; He is just and having salvation, lowly and riding on a donkey, a colt, the foal of a donkey.'**[57]

Also we can read the prophecy in Zephaniah about the coming of the King.

> **'Sing, O daughter of Zion! Shout, O Israel! Be glad and rejoice with all your heart, O daughter of Jerusalem! The LORD has taken away your judgements, He has cast out your enemy. The King of Israel, the LORD, is in your midst.'**[58]

Meditate on the humility, and see that Jesus was preparing a different way to be the Messiah. He would suffer on the cross to gain salvation for the whole world, not just the Jews.

Hymn:

Ride on, ride on in majesty!
Hark, all the tribes hosanna cry;
O Saviour meek, pursue Thy road
With palms and scattered garments strowed.

Ride on, ride on in majesty!
In lowly pomp ride on to die;
O Christ Thy triumphs. now begin
O'er captive death and conquered sin.

Ride on, ride on in majesty!
The angel hosts beyond the sky
Look down with sad and wondering eyes
To see the approaching sacrifice.

Ride on, ride on in majesty!
Thy last and fiercest strife is nigh;
The Father on the sapphire throne
Expects Thee, loved, anointed Son.

Ride on, ride on in majesty!
In lowly pomp ride on to die;
Bow Thy meek head to mortal pain,
Then take, O God, Thy power and reign.[59]

Prayer:

Receive Jesus into your life with humility, as the suffering servant of God.

Pray that one day the whole world will greet Him with Praise and Adoration.

Meditation 39: Washing the Disciples' Feet

John Chapter 13: 1 - 17

Now before the Feast of the Passover, when Jesus knew that His hour had come that He should depart from this world to the Father, having loved His own who were in the world, He loved them to the end.

And supper being ended, the devil having already put it into the heart of Judas Iscariot, Simon's son, to betray Him, Jesus, knowing that the Father had given all things into His hands, and that He had come from God and was going to God, rose from supper and laid aside His garments, took a towel and girded Himself. After that, He poured water into a basin and began to wash the disciples' feet, and to wipe them with the towel with which He was girded. Then He came to Simon Peter. And Peter said to Him, "Lord, are you washing my feet?"

Jesus answered and said to him, "What I am doing you do not understand now, but you will know after this." Peter said to Him, "You shall never wash my feet!" Jesus answered him, "If I do not wash you, you have no part with Me." Simon Peter said to Him, "Lord, not my feet only, but also my hands and my head!" Jesus said to him, "He who is bathed needs only to wash his feet, but is completely clean; and you are clean, but not all of you." For He knew who would betray Him; therefore He said, "You are not all clean."

So when He had washed their feet, taken His garments, and sat down again, He said to them, "Do you know what I have done to you? You call Me Teacher and Lord, and you say well, for so I am. If then, your Lord and Teacher, have washed your feet, you also ought to wash one another's feet. For I have given you an example, that you should do as I have done to you. Most assuredly, I say to you, a servant is not greater than his master, nor is he who is sent greater than he who sent him. If you know these things, blessed are you if you do them."

Picture the whole scene in the house where Jesus takes the basin of water, which was the duty of the lowest servant in any house, to wash the feet of a guest who had, perhaps, walked into the house with sand on his feet.

Reflect on the fact that Jesus did this knowing who He was - the Son of God - where He had come from - Heaven and the presence of His Father, and where He was going - to Glory.

Reflect on His great humility; see Him washing the disciples' feet. See and hear Peter's refusal to allow Him to do so because he realised that he should be washing Jesus' feet, not vice versa.

Hear Jesus' words of command as He, the greatest one, the Messiah, had washed the disciples' feet, so also His followers should wash each other's feet in humility.

Ponder that humility was a cardinal mark of Jesus' followers in their life together for all time.

Hymn:

Christian hearts in love united,
Search to know God's holy will.
Let His love, in us ignited,
More and more our spirits fill.
Christ the head, and we His members;
We reflect the light He is.
Christ the master, we disciples;
He is ours and we are His.

Grant, Lord, that with your direction
'Love each other' we comply.
Help us live in true affection,
Your love to exemplify.
Let our mutual love be glowing
Brightly so that all may view
That we, as on one stem growing,
Living branches are in You.

Come, then, living church of Jesus,
Covenant with Him anew.
Unto Him who conquered for use
May we pledge our service true.
May our lives reflect the brightness
Of God's love in Jesus shown.
To the world we then bear witness:
We belong to God alone.[60]

Prayer:

Ask God that He will grant the grace of humility in your own life and in your relationship with others and ponder any time when you have been unduly proud to safeguard your position in the church or society.

Pray that humility will, even today, be the mark of Jesus' people in their communal life in the church.

Meditation 40: The Last Supper

Matthew Chapter 26: 26

> **And as they were eating, Jesus took bread, blessed and broke it, and gave it to the disciples and said, "Take eat; this is My body." Then He took the cup, and gave thanks, and gave it to them, saying, "Drink from it, all of you. For this is My blood of the new covenant, which is shed for many for the remission of sins. But I say to you, I will not drink of this fruit of the vine from now on until that day when I drink it new with you in My Father's kingdom."**

Picture the upper room where Jesus knew He would eat His last meal with the disciples before His crucifixion.

See the disciples around the table. See Jesus breaking the bread and pouring the wine and hear His words about this being the sign of the institution by God of the New Covenant, a covenant of forgiveness of sins, written on believers' hearts.

Hear Him identify the bread as symbolising His body and the wine symbolising His blood. As you do this remember it was a very solemn occasion, and the institution of a simple meal which Jesus' followers would re-enact very often until Jesus would return in glory.

Hymn:

> And now, O Father, mindful of the love
> That bought us, once for all, on Calvary's tree,
> And having with us Him that pleads above,
> We here present, we have spread forth to Thee
> That only offering perfect in Thine eyes,
> The one true, pure, immortal sacrifice.
>
> Look, Father, look on His anointed face,
> And only look on us as found in Him;
> Look not on our misusing of Thy grace,
> Our prayer so languid, and our faith so dim:
> For lo, between our sins and their reward
> We set the Passion of Thy Son our Lord.
>
> And so we come: O draw us to Thy feet,
> Most patient Saviour, who canst love us still;
> And by this food, so awful and so sweet,
> Deliver us from every touch of ill:
> In Thine own service make us glad and free,
> And grant us never more to part with Thee.[61]

Prayer:

Remember that you, as a baptised Christian, have been able to partake of this meal with solemnity, confessing any sins you have, claiming God's forgiveness and rededicating yourself to His service.

Meditation 41: The Garden of Gethsemane

Matthew Chapter 26: 36-46

Then Jesus came with them to a place called Gethsemane, and said to the disciples, "Sit here while I go and pray over there." And He took with Him Peter and the two sons of Zebedee, and He began to be sorrowful and deeply distressed. Then He said to them, "My soul is exceedingly sorrowful, even to death. Stay here and watch with Me" He went a little farther and fell on His face, and prayed, saying, "O My Father, if it is possible, let this cup pass from Me, nevertheless, not as I will, but as You will."
Then He came to the disciples and found them sleeping and said to Peter, "What? Could you not watch with Me one hour? Watch and pray, lest you enter into temptation. The spirit indeed is willing, but the flesh is weak."

Again, the second time, He went away and prayed, saying, "O My Father, if this cup cannot pass away from Me unless I drink it, Your will be done." And He came and found them asleep again, for their eyes were heavy. So He left them, went away again, and prayed the third time, saying the same words. Then He came to His disciples and said to them, "Are you still sleeping and resting? Behold, the hour is at hand, and the Son of Man is being betrayed into the hands of sinners. Rise, let us be going. See, My betrayer is at hand."

And while He was still speaking, behold, Judas, one of the twelve, with a great multitude with swords and clubs, came from the chief priests and elders of the people. Now His betrayer had given them a sign, saying, "Whomever I kiss, He is the One, seize Him." Immediately he went up to Jesus and said, "Greetings, Rabbi!" and kissed Him. But Jesus said to him, "Friend, why have you come?"

Then they came and laid hands on Jesus and took Him. And suddenly, one of those who were with Jesus stretched out his hand and drew his sword, struck the servant of the high priest, and cut off his ear. But Jesus said to him, "Put your sword in its place, for all who take the sword will perish by the sword. Or do you think that I cannot now pray to My Father, and He will provide Me with more than twelve legions of angels? How then could the Scriptures be fulfilled, that it must happen thus?" In that hour Jesus said to the multitudes, "Have you come out, as against a robber, with swords and clubs to take Me? I sat daily with you, teaching in the temple, and you did not seize Me. But all this was done that the Scriptures of the prophets might be fulfilled." Then all the disciples forsook Him and fled.

Reflect on the fact that the whole future of man's spiritual life or death hung in the balance as Jesus prayed in the garden.

It was night; so, picture the darkness.

Hear Jesus hoping His disciples would watch and pray with Him.

See Jesus lying on His face and three times uttering the same prayer, and see the disciples sleeping because they were so tired and hear Jesus' painful rebuking of them.

See the arrest of Jesus in its entirety and remember that human beings were arresting God.

Hymn:

> **Praise to the Holiest in the height,**
> **And in the depth be praise:**
> **In all His words most wonderful,**
> **Most sure in all His ways.**
>
> **O loving wisdom of our God,**
> **When all was sin and shame,**
> **He, the last Adam, to the fight**
> **And to the rescue came.**
>
> **O wisest love! That flesh and blood**
> **Which did in Adam fail,**
> **Should strive afresh against the foe,**
> **Should strive and should prevail.**

And that a higher gift than grace
Should flesh and blood refine,
God's presence, and His very self
And essence all-divine.

O generous love! That He, who smote
In man for man the foe,
The double agony in man
For man should undergo.

And in the garden secretly,
And on the cross on high,
Should teach His brethren, and inspire
To suffer and to die.

Praise to the Holiest in the height,
And in the depth be praise:
In all His words most wonderful,
Most sure in all His ways.[62]

Prayer:

Reflect on any time when you have failed in a needful prayer time for any one or any cause.

Ask God to strengthen you to be a person of prayer, knowing that in this you are cooperating with God in the salvation of humanity.

Meditation 42: Jesus Crucified

John Chapter 19: 17 – 42

And He, bearing His cross, went out to a place called the Place of a Skull, which is called in Hebrew, Golgotha, where they crucified Him, and two others with Him, one on either side, and Jesus in the centre. Now Pilate wrote a title and put it on the cross. And the writing was: **JESUS OF NAZARETH, THE KING OF THE JEWS.** Then many of the Jews read this title, for the place where Jesus was crucified was near the city; and it was written in Hebrew, Greek, and Latin. Therefore the chief priests of the Jews said to Pilate, "Do not write, 'The King of the Jews,' but, 'He said, "I am the King of the Jews."'" Pilate answered, "What I have written, I have written."
Then the soldiers, when they had crucified Jesus, took His garments and made four parts, to each soldier a part, and also the tunic. Now the tunic was without seam, woven from the top in one piece. They said therefore among themselves, "Let us not tear it, but cast lots for it, whose it shall be," that the Scripture might be fulfilled which says: "They divided My garments among them, And for my clothing they cast lots." Therefore the soldiers did these things.

Now there stood by the cross of Jesus His mother, and His mother's sister, Mary the wife of Clopas, and Mary Magdalene. When Jesus therefore saw His mother, and the disciple whom He loved standing by, He said to His mother, "Woman behold your son!" Then He said to the disciple, "Behold your mother!" And from that hour the disciple took her to his own home.

After this, Jesus, knowing that all things were now accomplished, that the Scripture might be fulfilled, said, "I thirst!" Now a vessel full of sour wine was sitting there; and they filled a sponge with sour wine, put it on hyssop, and put it to His mouth. So when Jesus had received the sour wine, He said, "It is finished!" And bowing His head, He gave up His spirit. Therefore, because it was the Preparation Day, that the bodies should not remain on the cross on the Sabbath (for that Sabbath was a high day), the Jews asked Pilate that their legs might be broken, and that they might be taken away. Then the soldiers came and broke the legs of the first and of the other who was crucified with Him. But when they came to Jesus and saw that He was already dead, they did not break His legs. But one of the soldiers pierced His side, with a spear, and immediately blood and water came out. And he who has seen has testified, and his testimony is true; and he knows that he is telling the truth, so that you may believe. For these things were done that the Scripture should be fulfilled, "Not one of His bones shall be broken." And again another Scripture says "They shall look on Him whom they pierced."

Picture the whole graphic scene of the three crosses on the hill of Golgotha with Jesus in the middle of the two robbers.

See Him there and hear all the words He said on the cross.

Read Psalm 22, which prophetically and graphically foretells the Lord's crucifixion.

2 Corinthian Chapter 5: 18-19

> **Now all things are of God, who has reconciled us to Himself through Jesus Christ, and has given us the ministry of reconciliation, that is, that God was in Christ, reconciling the world to Himself, not imputing their trespasses to them, and has committed to us the word of reconciliation.**

Hymn:

> **When I survey the wondrous cross**
> **On which the Prince of glory died,**
> **My richest gain I count but loss,**
> **And pour contempt on all my pride.**
>
> **Forbid it, Lord, that I should boast**
> **Save in the death of Christ, my God!**
> **All the vain things that charm me most,**
> **I sacrifice them through His blood.**

See, from His head, His hands, His feet,
Sorrow and love flow mingled down.
Did e'er such love and sorrow meet,
Or thorns compose so rich a crown?

Were the whole realm of nature mine,
That were an offering far too small
Love so amazing, so divine,
Demands my soul, my life, my all.[63]

Prayer:

Pray with great solemnity and thanksgiving.

See that in this wondrous yet terrible event, God's plan of saving the human race was finished, as in the words of Jesus, "It is finished". It is completed - it is perfected.

Thank God for saving you.

There is a fountain filled with blood
Drawn from Immanuel's veins;
And sinners plunged beneath that flood,
lose all their guilty stains.[64]

Glory be to Jesus,
Who, in bitter pains
Poured for me the lifeblood
From His sacred veins.

Lift we, then, our voices,
Swell the mighty flood,
Louder still and louder,
praise the precious blood.[65]

Meditation 43: The Morning of the Resurrection

John Chapter 20: 1 - 18

Now on the first day of the week Mary Magdalene went to the tomb early, while it was still dark, and saw that the stone had been taken away from the tomb. Then she ran and came to Simon Peter, and to the other disciple, whom Jesus loved, and said to them, "They have taken away the Lord out of the tomb, and we do not know where they have laid Him."
Peter therefore went out, and the other disciple, and were going to the tomb. So they both ran together, and the other disciple outran Peter and came to the tomb first. And he, stooping down and looking in, saw the linen cloths lying there; yet he did not go in. Then Simon Peter came, following him, and went into the tomb; and he saw the linen cloths lying there, and the handkerchief that had been around His head, not lying with the linen cloths, but folded together in a place by itself. Then the other disciple, who came to the tomb first, went in also; and he saw and believed. For as yet they did not know the Scripture, that He must rise again from the dead. Then the disciples went away again to their own homes.

But Mary stood outside by the tomb weeping, and as she wept, she stooped down and looked into the tomb. And she saw two angels in white sitting, one at the head and the other at the

feet, where the body of Jesus had lain. Then they said to her, "Woman, why are you weeping?" She said to them, "Because they have taken away my Lord, and I do not know where they have laid Him."

Now when she had said this, she turned around and saw Jesus standing there, and did not know that it was Jesus. Jesus said to her, "Woman, why are you weeping? Whom are you seeking?" She, supposing Him to be the gardener, said to Him, "Sir, if You have carried Him away, tell me where You have laid Him, and I will take Him away." Jesus said to her, "Mary!" She turned and said to Him, "Rabboni!" (which is to say, Teacher). Jesus said to her, "Do not cling to Me, for I have not yet ascended to My Father; but go to My brethren and say to them, 'I am ascending to My Father and your Father, and to My God and your God'." Mary Magdalene came and told the disciples that she had seen the Lord, and that He had spoken these things to her.

Feel the wonder, the surprise, the disbelief and finally, the wonderful realisation that the Lord was risen!

Hear the early Christians' call on Easter morning:

"The Lord is Risen - The Lord is Risen indeed!"

Hymn:

Thine be the Glory, risen conquering Son
Endless is the victory Thou o'er death has won;
Angels in bright raiment rolled the stone away,
Kept the folded grave clothes where Thy body
lay.
Thine be the glory risen conquering Son,
Endless is the victory Thou o'er death hast won.

Lo! Jesus meets us, risen from the tomb;
Lovingly He greets us, scatters fear and gloom.
Let the Church with gladness hymns of triumph
sing,
For her Lord now liveth; death has lost its sting.
Thine be the glory risen conquering Son,
Endless is the victory, Thou o'er death hast won.

No more we doubt Thee, glorious Prince of Life;
Life is nought without Thee: aid us in our strife.
Make us more than conquerors through Thy
deathless love;
Bring us safe through Jordan to Thy home
above.
Thine be the glory risen conquering Son,
Endless is the victory, Thou o'er death hast
won.[66]

Hallelujah, Amen.

Prayer:

Take the Risen Lord again into your life, and dedicate yourself to sharing, wherever you can, the Good News of the resurrection and the end of death's dominion.

Meditation 44: The Ascension

Acts Chapter 1: 1 - 11

The former account I made, O Theophilus, of all that Jesus began both to do and teach, until the day in which He was taken up, after He through the Holy Spirit had given commandments to the apostles whom He had chosen, to whom also He presented Himself alive after His suffering by many infallible proofs, being seen by them during forty days and speaking of the things pertaining to the kingdom of God.
And being assembled together with them, He commanded them not to depart from Jerusalem, but to wait for the promise of the Father, "which", He said, "you have heard from Me; for John truly baptised with water, but you shall be baptised with the Holy Spirit not many days from now." Therefore, when they had come together, they asked Him, saying, "Lord, will You at this time restore the kingdom to Israel?" And He said to them, "It is not for you to know times or seasons which the Father has put in His own authority. But you shall receive power when the Holy Spirit has come upon you; and you shall be witnesses to Me in Jerusalem, and in all Judea and Samaria, and to the end of the earth."
Now when He had spoken these things, while they watched, He was taken up, and a cloud received Him out of their sight. And while they looked steadfastly toward heaven as He went

up, behold, two men stood by them in white apparel, who also said, "Men of Galilee, why do you stand gazing up into heaven? This same Jesus who was taken up from you into heaven, will so come in like manner as you saw Him go into heaven."

Picture this whole scene in deeds and words, and in your imagination, see the Lord ascending in the great cloud.

Hymn:

> **Hail to the Lord's Anointed,**
> **great David's greater Son!**
> **Hail in the time appointed,**
> **His reign on earth begun!**
> **He comes to break oppression,**
> **to set the captive free,**
> **To take away transgression**
> **and rule in equity.**
>
> **To Him shall prayer unceasing**
> **And daily vows ascend;**
> **His kingdom still increasing,**
> **A kingdom without end.**
> **The tide of time shall never**
> **His covenant remove;**
> **His name shall stand forever;**
> **That name to us is Love.**[67]

Prayer:
Praise and adore the ascended Lord of Glory.
Thank Him for His victory over sin and death and rededicate yourself to serve the King of Kings.

Meditation 45: The Glorification of Jesus Christ

Revelation Chapter 7: 9 - 12

After these things I looked, and behold, a great multitude which no one could number, of all nations, tribes, peoples, and tongues, standing before the throne and before the Lamb, clothed with white robes, with palm branches in their hands, and crying out with a loud voice, saying, "Salvation belongs to our God who sits on the throne, and to the Lamb!" All the angels stood around the throne and the elders and the four living creatures, and fell on their faces before the throne and worshipped God, saying, "Amen! Blessing and glory and wisdom, thanksgiving and honour and power and might, be to our God forever and ever. Amen."

Worship the Lord, the Lamb of God, crucified, risen, and now glorified.

Try to be one the elders worshipping Him using the same words as they did.

Hymn:

Glorious things of Thee are spoken,
Zion, city of our God;
He whose word cannot be broken
Formed thee for His own abode;
On the Rock of Ages founded,
What can shake the sure repose?
With salvations' walls surrounded,
Thou mays't smile at all Thy foes.

See the streams of living waters,
Springing from eternal love,
Well supply Thy sons and daughters,
And all fear of want remove;
Who can faint while such a river
Ever flows their thirst t'assuage?
Grace, which like the Lord, the giver,
Never fails from age to age.[68]

Prayer:

Crown Him again as the Lord of your life; worship, adore, and dedicate yourselves to His service.

Determine to live your life in obedience to Him as the ruler of it.

PART THREE

Devotions related to aspects of the person and work of the Holy Spirit

Meditation 46: The Holy Spirit Active in our New Birth

John Chapter 3: 1 - 13

There was a man of the Pharisees named Nicodemus, a ruler of the Jews. This man came to Jesus by night and said to Him, "Rabbi, we know that You are a teacher come from God; for no one can do these signs that You do unless God is with him." Jesus answered and said to him, "Most assuredly, I say to you, unless one is born again, he cannot see the kingdom of God." Nicodemus said to Him, "How can a man be born when he is old? Can he enter a second time into his mother's womb and be born?"

Jesus answered, "Most assuredly, I say to you, unless one is born of water and the Spirit, he cannot enter the kingdom of God. That which is born of the flesh is flesh, and that which is born of the Spirit is spirit. Do not marvel that I said to you, 'You must be born again.' The wind blows where it wishes, and you hear the sound of it, but cannot tell where it comes from and where it goes. So is everyone who is born of the Spirit."

Nicodemus answered and said to Him, "How can these things be?" Jesus answered and said to him, "Are you the teacher of Israel, and do not know these things? Most assuredly, I say to you, We speak what We know and testify what We have seen, and you do not receive Our witness. If I have told you earthly things and you do not believe, how will you believe if I tell

you heavenly things? No one has ascended to heaven but He who came down from heaven, that is, the Son of Man who is in heaven.

Have you experienced the new birth? When did this happen? Were you aware of this as a new experience of the kingdom of God?

Jesus says that you need to be born again even to see the kingdom of God. Have you spiritually seen it?

Hymn:

> **Amazing grace, how sweet the sound,**
> **That saved a wretch like me.**
> **I once was lost but now am found,**
> **Was blind, but now I see.**
>
> **'Twas grace that taught my heart to fear**
> **And grace my fears relieved.**
> **How precious did that grace appear**
> **The hour I first believed.**
>
> **Through many dangers, toils, and snares**
> **I have already come;**
> **'Twas grace that brought me safe thus far**
> **And grace will lead me home.**[69]

Prayer:
Thank God for this wonderful experience given you by the Holy Spirit. Praise the Lord that through this you are now a citizen in the Kingdom of God. Pray for others, even church goers you know, who have not had this experience.

Meditation 47: Jesus Gives the Holy Spirit to the Disciples

John Chapter 20: 19-23

> **Then, the same day at evening, being the first day of the week, when the doors were shut and where the disciples were assembled, for fear of the Jews, Jesus came and stood in the midst, and said to them, "Peace be with you." When He had said this, He showed them His hands and His side. Then the disciples were glad when they saw the Lord.**
> **So Jesus said to them again, "Peace to you! As the Father has sent Me, I also send you." And when He had said this, He breathed on them, and said to them, "Receive the Holy Spirit. If you forgive the sins of any, they are forgiven them; if you retain the sins of any, they are retained."**

We need to receive the Holy Spirit into our lives as a definite experience of God's gift to us.

We need constantly, even daily, to renew this experience of breathing in, even physically, but certainly spiritually, the Holy Spirit.

Seek, and receive, the Holy Spirit early in the morning so that His presence will be with us at all times during the day.

Hymn:

Breathe on me, breath of God,
Fill me with life anew,
That I may love what Thou dost love,
And do what Thou wouldst do.

Breathe on me, breath of God,
Until my heart is pure,
Until with Thee I will one will,
To do and to endure.

Breathe on me, Breath of God
Till I am wholly Thine,
Until this earthly part of me,
Glows with Thy fire divine.

Breathe on me, breath of God
So shall I never die,
But live with Thee the perfect life
Of Thine eternity.[70]

Prayer:

Pray that you will receive the Holy Spirit; that you will receive Him now.

Pray that Jesus will 'breathe' on you as He did with His first disciples and that you will be able to 'breathe in' that Breath of God into the deepest reaches of your being.

Meditation 48: The Convicting Work of the Holy Spirit

John Chapter 16: 5 -15

> "But now I go away to Him who sent Me, and none of you asks Me, 'Where are You going? But because I have said these things to you, sorrow has filled your heart. Nevertheless I tell you the truth. It is to your advantage that I go away; for if I do not go away, the Helper will not come to you; but if I depart, I will send Him to you. And when He has come, He will convict the world of sin, and of righteousness, and of judgement: of sin, because they do not believe in Me; of righteousness, because I go to My Father and you see Me no more; of judgement, because the ruler of this world is judged. I still have many things to say to you, but you cannot bear them now. However, when He, the Spirit of truth, has come, He will guide you into all truth; for He will not speak on His own authority, but whatever He hears He will speak; and He will tell you things to come. He will glorify Me, for He will take of what is Mine and declare it to you."

We need to be convicted of sin: of thought, word, and deed, of things done and left undone.

Conviction means an inner feeling, even of agony over this sin.

Hymn:

Sinners Jesus will receive
Sound this word of grace to all
Who the heavenly pathway leave,
All who linger, all who fall.

> **Refrain:**
> **Sing it o'er and o'er again:**
> **Christ receiveth sinful men.**
> **Make the message clear and plain;**
> **Christ receiveth sinful men.**

Come, and He will give you rest;
Trust Him, for His word is plain;
He will take the sinfulest;
Christ receiveth sinful men.

Now my heart condemns me not,
Pure before the law I stand;
He who cleansed me from all spot
Satisfied its last demand.

Christ receiveth sinful men,
Even me with all my sin;
Purged from every spot and stain,
Glory I shall enter in.[71]

Prayer:

Pray that when the Holy Spirit needs to convict you of sin, in order that you may receive the Lord's forgiveness, you will not 'harden your heart' but be responsive to His movement in your life.

Meditation 49: The Promise of the Ascended Lord

Acts Chapter 1: 4 - 8

> **And being assembled together with them, He commanded them not to depart from Jerusalem, but to wait for the Promise of the Father, "which", He said, "you have heard from Me, for John truly baptised with water, but you shall be baptised with the Holy Spirit not many days from now." Therefore, when they had come together, they asked Him, saying, "Lord, will You at this time restore the kingdom to Israel?" And He said to them, "It is not for you to know the times or seasons which the Father has put in His own authority. But you shall receive power when the Holy Spirit has come upon you; and you shall be witnesses to Me in Jerusalem, and in all Judea and Samaria, and to the end of the earth."**

The word 'baptism' means to be immersed, in this case immersed in the Holy Spirit to receive His power.

Note that this promise comes after Jesus has breathed on His disciples and they received the Holy Spirit. It is a separate experience for a believer after being born again.

Have you experienced the baptism of the Holy Spirit? If not, pray that you may do so.

Hymn:

> **Come, Holy Ghost, Creator blest,**
> **And in our hearts take up Thy rest;**
> **Come with Thy grace and heavenly aid**
> **To fill the hearts which Thou hast made.**
>
> **O Comforter, to Thee we cry,**
> **Thou heavenly gift of God most high,**
> **Thou fount of life, and fire of love,**
> **And sweet anointing from above.**
>
> **O Holy Ghost, through Thee alone**
> **Know we the Father and the Son**
> **Be this our firm unchanging creed,**
> **That Thou dost from them both proceed.**
>
> **Praise we the Lord, Father and Son,**
> **And Holy Spirit with them one;**
> **And may the Son on us bestow**
> **All gifts that from the Spirit flow.**[72]

Prayer:

Spirit of the living God fall afresh on me. Mould me, fill me, use me.

Meditation 50: The Holy Spirit Given for us to Witness

Luke Chapter 24: 48-49

"And you are witnesses of these things. Behold, I send the Promise of My Father upon you; but tarry in the city of Jerusalem until you are endued with power from on high."

A witness is someone who can describe an event not from second-hand knowledge but as a personal experience.

This is the experience that made the change in our life which has happened, because of the presence of the Holy Spirit in us.

We are meant to be witnesses of the fact that Jesus is alive in us.

Hymn:

**O Jesus, I have promised
to serve Thee to the end;
Be Thou forever near me.
My Master and my Friend;
I shall not fear the battle
if Thou art by my side,
Nor wander from the pathway
if Thou wilt be my Guide.**

Oh, let me feel Thee near me,
the world is ever near;
I see the sights that dazzle,
the tempting sounds I hear.
My foes are ever near me,
around me and within;
But, Jesus, draw Thou nearer,
and shield my soul from sin.

Oh, let me see Thy footmarks
and in them plant my own.
My hope to follow duly
is in Thy strength alone;
Oh, guide me, call me, draw me,
uphold me to the end
And then in heaven receive me,
My Saviour and my Friend.[73]

Prayer:

Ask the Lord for forgiveness for any time when you have had the opportunity but have failed to witness to the change that Jesus has wrought in your life.

Rededicate yourself to be a witness, not only by what you say, but by the way you live, and pray that you may be used to win others for the Lord's kingdom.

Meditation 51: Jesus' Promise of the Holy Spirit

John Chapter 14: 15 - 18

> **"If you love Me, keep My commandments. And I will pray the Father, and He will give you another Helper, that He may abide with you forever - the Spirit of truth, whom the world cannot receive, because it neither sees Him nor knows Him; but you know Him, for He dwells with you and will be in you. I will not leave you orphans; I will come to you."**

Thank the Lord for His promise to send to His disciples, and down the years to you, another Helper. (The Greek word Paraclete - does not mean 'comforter' as we know that word today, the word Divine Helper is a much better translation).

Thank Jesus for this promise to follow His departure to heaven.

Have you consciously received this gift of the Holy Spirit into your life? If so, when and what difference has He made?

(The Holy Spirit is a person, not a sort of indefinite spirit. The Holy Spirit is talked about by Jesus as 'He').

Hymn:

O come and dwell in me,
Spirit of power within,
And bring the glorious liberty
from sorrow, fear, and sin.

Hasten the joyful day
which shall my sins consume,
When old things shall be done away,
and all thing new become.

I want the witness, Lord,
that all I do is right,
According to thy mind and word,
Well-pleasing in Thy sight.

I ask no higher state;
indulge me but in this,
And soon or later then translate
to Thine eternal bliss.[74]

Prayer:

Thank God for the gift of the Holy Spirit in your life and pray: 'Still stir up the gift in me, ready for all Thy perfect will, my acts of faith and love repeat.'[75]

When did you last pray to the Holy Spirit to help you?

Meditation 52: The Fruit of the Holy Spirit

Galatians Chapter 5: 22 -23

> **But the fruit of the spirit is love, joy, peace, longsuffering, kindness, goodness, faithfulness, gentleness, self-control. Against such there is no law.**

These are the essential virtues of the Christian life, in themselves a total picture of the beauty of Jesus.

Read them all carefully and pray that each one may be present in your life.

Matthew Chapter 7:16-20

> **"You will know them by their fruits. Do men gather grapes from thornbushes or figs from thistles? Even so, every good tree bears good fruit, but a bad tree bears bad fruit. A good tree cannot bear bad fruit, nor can a bad tree bear good fruit. Every tree that does not bear good fruit is cut down and thrown into the fire. Therefore by their fruits you will know them."**

Hymn:

Gracious Spirit, dwell with me;
I myself would gracious be;
And with words that help and heal
Would Thy life in mine reveal;
And with actions bold and meek
Would for Christ my Saviour speak.

Truthful Spirit, dwell with me;
I myself would truthful be;
And with wisdom kind and clear
Let Thy life in mine appear
And with actions brotherly
Speak my Lord's sincerity.

Holy Spirit, dwell with me;
I myself would holy be;
Separate from sin, I would
Choose and cherish all things good,
And whatever I can be,
Give to Him who gave me Thee.[76]

Prayer:

Pray that the beauty, compassion, and purity of Jesus will be seen in you, realising that you cannot produce this fruit yourself.

Pray that the Holy Spirit may be at work in you to this end; to produce these beautiful fruits in your character as a Christian.

Meditation 53: The Holy Spirit Bringing us into All Truth

John Chapter 14:26

> **"But the Helper, the Holy Spirit, whom the Father will send in My name, He will teach you all things, and bring to your remembrance all things that I said to you."**

1 Corinthians Chapter 2:12-13

> **Now we have received, not the spirit of the world, but the Spirit who is from God, that we might know the things that have been freely given to us by God. These things we also speak, not in words which man's wisdom teaches but which the Holy Spirit teaches, comparing spiritual things with spiritual.**

Meditate on the fact that truth is not a lot of propositions but is all contained ultimately in the person of our Lord Jesus Christ Consider what truth you have been shown and how your life through the Holy Spirit may glorify Jesus.

Therefore, God has highly exalted Him and given Him the name, which is above every name, that at the name of Jesus every knee should bow, of those in heaven, and of those on earth, and of those under the earth, and that every tongue should confess that Jesus Christ is Lord, to the glory of God the Father.

Hymn:

At the name of Jesus
every knee shall bow,
Every tongue confess Him
King of Glory now.
'Tis the Father's pleasure
we should call Him Lord,
Who from the beginning
was the mighty Word.

In your hearts enthrone Him;
there let Him subdue
All that is not holy,
All that is not true;
Crown Him as your Captain
in temptation's hour:
Let His will enfold you
in its light and power.

Brothers, this Lord Jesus
shall return again,
With His Father's glory,
with His angel train;
For all wreaths of empire
meet upon His brow,
And out hearts confess Him
King of Glory now.[77]

Prayer:
Confess when your life has in any way glorified yourself and not Jesus. Pray that you may indeed, be entering into more and more truth, and thank God that He has revealed this to you through the Holy Spirit and pray that your life may glorify the risen Lord.

PART FOUR

Conclusion

Meditation 54: The Holy Trinity
God the Father, God the Son, God the Holy Spirit

1 Peter Chapter 1:1

> **To the pilgrims of the Dispersion in Pontus, Galatia, Cappadocia, Asia, and Bithynia, elect according to the foreknowledge of God the Father, in sanctification of the Spirit, for obedience and sprinkling of the blood of Jesus Christ.**

We have experienced the one God in three Persons as set forth in this verse.

Meditate on each Person of the Trinity and examine where each has worked His spiritual work in your life.

Hymn:

> **Holy, holy, holy! Lord God Almighty!**
> **Early in the morning**
> **our song shall rise to Thee.**
> **Holy, holy, holy! Merciful and mighty!**
> **God in three persons, blessed Trinity!**
>
> **Holy, holy, holy! Though the darkness hide Thee**
> **Though the eye of sinful man**
> **Thy glory may not see,**
> **Only Thou art holy; there is none beside Thee,**
> **Perfect in power, in love, and purity.**

Holy, holy, holy! Lord God Almighty!
All Thy works shall praise Thy name,
in earth and sky and sea,
Holy, holy, holy! Merciful and mighty!
God in three persons, blessed Trinity![78]

Prayer:

Thank God that you know Him in all His fullness, yet in a mystery.

Rededicate yourself to the service of God by praying the Lord's prayer.

Matthew Chapter 6: 9 -14

Our Father in heaven,
Hallowed be Your name.
Your kingdom come.
Your will be done
On earth as it is in heaven.
Give us this day our daily bread.
And forgive us our debts,
As we forgive our debtors.
And do not lead us into temptation,
But deliver us from the evil one.
For Yours is the kingdom and the power
and the glory forever.
AMEN.

Suggested Prayers

Opening Prayer:

Almighty God to whom all hearts are open, all desires known, and from no secrets are hid, cleanse the thoughts of our hearts by the inspiration of Your Holy Spirit, that we might perfectly love You, and worthily magnify Your Holy name, through Jesus Christ our Lord, Amen.

Father of all, we thank You for our creation, preservation, and all the blessings of this life, but above all, we thank You for Your inestimable love in the redemption of the world by our Lord Jesus Christ, who is the image of God, for the means of Grace and the Hope of glory, and we ask that we may show forth our praise, not only by the words of our lips, but by the manner of our lives, by giving up ourselves to your service and walking before You in holiness and righteousness all our days. Through Jesus Christ our Lord. Amen.

A prayer of confession:

O Lord God, our Heavenly Father, we confess that we have sinned against you in thought, word, and deed, by what we have done, and by what we have left undone, and we confess that we have not loved our neighbours as ourselves. Have mercy upon us most merciful Lord. Pardon and deliver us from all our sins, amendment of life, and the grace and comfort of the Holy Spirit. Though Jesus Christ our Lord. Amen

Suggested Closing Hymn

O God, our help in ages past,
Our hope for years to come,
Our shelter from the stormy blast,
And our eternal home.

Beneath the shadow of Thy throne,
Thy saints have dwelt secure,
Sufficient is Thy arm alone,
And our defence is sure.

Before the hills in order stood,
Or earth received her frame,
From everlasting Thou art God,
To endless years the same.

A thousand ages in Thy sight
Are like an evening gone,
Short as the watch that ends the night
Before the rising sun.

Time, like an ever-rolling stream,
Bears all its sons away.
They fly, forgotten, as a dream
Dies at the opening day.

O God, our help in ages past,
Our hope for years to come,
Be Thou our guide while troubles last,
And our eternal home![79]

The Apostle's Creed

A very early statement of what Christians believed in the first century AD.

I believe in God,
the Father Almighty,
Creator of heaven and earth,
and in Jesus Christ, His only Son, our Lord,
who was conceived by the Holy Spirit,
born of the Virgin Mary,
suffered under Pontius Pilate,
was crucified, dead, and was buried;
He descended into hell;
on the third day He rose again from the dead;
He ascended into heaven,
and is seated at the right hand of God the Father almighty;
from there He will come again to judge both the living and the dead.

I believe in the Holy Spirit,
the Holy Catholic and Apostolic Church,
the communion of saints,
the forgiveness of sins,
the resurrection of the body,
And life everlasting.
Amen.

References:

[1] John 10:27
[2] John 10:5
[3] John 10:7
[4] Matthew 6:31-33
[5] Joel 2:25
[6] Matthew 5:6
[7] Romans 8:37
[8] John14:2-3
[9] James Montgomery (1835)
[10] James 4:8
[11] Author: Joachim Neander (1680); Translator: Catherine Winkworth (1863)
[12] Walter C Smith (1867)
[13] Robert Grant (1833)
[14] Charles Wesley (1749)
[15] Psalm 145:13
[16] Charles Wesley (1747)
[17] Titus 2:11
[18] Samuel Davies (1723-1761)
[19] Frederick William Faber (1862)
[20] Horatius Bonar (1846)
[21] 1 Samuel 3:10
[22] Revelation 21:4
[23] John Newton (1779)
[24] Arthur Campbell Ainger (1894)
[25] Frances R Havergal (1872)
[26] James Edmeston (1821)
[27] Author: Martin Rinkart (1636); Translator: Catherine Winkworth (1829-78)
[28] Matthew Bridges (1851)
[29] Nahum Tate (1700)
[30] Charles Wesley (1745)
[31] John Samuel Bewley Monsell (1811-75)
[32] William Walsham How (1867)
[33] Edwin Hatch (1878)
[34] John Keble (1819)
[35] Cecil Francis Alexander (1852)
[36] John Ernest Bode (1869)
[37] John Newton (1779)
[38] Rufus H McDaniel (1914)
[39] Mary A Lathbury (1877)
[40] W O Cushing (1876)
[41] Charles Wesley (1740)

[42] Henry Twells (1868)
[43] Charles Wesley (1738)
[44] 1 Corinthians 3:6
[45] Matthew 9:37-38
[46] Author: Matthias Claudius (1782); Translator: Jane M Campbell (1861)
[47] William J Kirkpatrick (1892)
[48] Robert Walmsley (1900)
[49] Charles Wesley (1762)
[50] Thomas Binney (1826)
[51] Cleland Boyd McAfee (1903)
[52] John Marriott (1813)
[53] George W Doane (1824)
[54] James Montgomery (1835)
[55] Isaac Watts (1719)
[56] Psalm 23:4
[57] Zechariah 9:9
[58] Zephaniah 3:14-15
[59] Henry Hart Milman (1827)
[60] Author: Nicolaus Ludwig, Graf von Zinzendorf; Translator: Frederick William Foster (1723)
[61] William Bright (1874)
[62] John Henry Newman (1865)
[63] Isaac Watts (1707)
[64] William Cowper (1772)
[65] Edward Caswell (1857)
[66] Author: Edmond Budry; Translator: Richard Birch Hoyle (1904)
[67] James Montgomery (1821)
[68] John Newton (1779)
[69] John Newton (1779)
[70] Edwin Hatch (1878)
[71] Author: Erdmann Neumeister (1718); Translator: Frances Bevan (1899)
[72] Author: Rabanus Maurus (c776-856); Translator: Edward Caswell (1814-1878)
[73] John Ernest Bode (1869)
[74] Charles Wesley (1762)
[75] Charles Wesley (1762)
[76] Thomas T Lynch (1855)
[77] Caroline M Noel (1870)
[78] Reginald Heber (1826)
[79] Isaac Watts (1719)